MW01194204

"Joshua is a bright light in the world; Not just because of his brilliance, but because of his transparency. Read this book and be inspired heart to heart from someone who has figured out how to change the world without pretending."

- Rory Vaden, NY Times Best Selling Auhor, *Take The Stairs*

HUSTLE

THE PEOPLE AT THE TOP OF THE MOUNTAIN DIDN'T FALL THERE

Joshua Medcalf

Cover design by Steph Ianni.
Edited by: Jacob Roman and Jamie Gilbert
Unless otherwise indicated, Scripture quotations are from: The Holy Bible, New International Version © 1973, 1984 by International Bible Society, used by permission of Zondervan Publishing House.

Contents

What Truly Matters

"Our greatest fear in life should not be of failure, our greatest fear should be of succeeding at things in life that don't really matter."
-Francis Chan

Every day, people head out the door believing that everything will be different if they can just achieve more, win more, or make more money. But if achievement hasn't filled that void to date, how is achieving more going to fill it in the future? Like thirsty people guzzling salt water, achievement only creates a greater desire for accomplishing more, dehydrating us of true satisfaction and fulfillment.

The question to think about is this: what do you want to be remembered for when you're gone? Will it be the money you've made, the titles you had, or the championships you won? Everyone we work with agrees that what's most important is the influence you've had on others, and who you became in the process. If that's what matters on our deathbed, shouldn't we focus on that today? My fear is that many people will get to the end of their life, and the top of the ladder, only to realize their ladder has been on the wrong building the whole time.

I hope I won't be one of them. My deepest hope and passion is that I will gain perspective in life on what truly matters and put my ladder on the right building, while encouraging others to do the same. Hustle is crucial, but putting first things first is vital.

**Love,
Joshua Medcalf**

"When you put first things first, second things are not suppressed, they increase." –C.S. Lewis

Introduction

Over the last thirty years, my life has taken some twists and turns that are so hard to believe that some people think I made them up.

Sometimes I wish I had, but I didn't.

The stories in this book are the cold, raw, and vulnerable stories of my journey. Today, I have some really cool perks to my life, and I get to do lots of amazing things, but becoming this resourceful, opportunistic person has been a serious journey, and I still struggle daily.

I wish I had learned many of these lessons an easier way, but hopefully you can learn from my mistakes, failures, and successes.

This is the book I wish someone would have given me 10 years ago, and said "This is your blueprint for making your dreams come true."

The people at the top of the mountain didn't fall there. Greatness always looks easy to those who aren't around when all the training happens.

Foreword

I remember it like it was yesterday. I had just taken the ball and I was running up along the boards of the indoor soccer field on my way to score. Out of the opposing team's box comes this clown who smashes me up against the boards. No words, no reaction, and no attempt to hit the ball. As I lay in a heap on the ground, I watched Bear just walk off the field and out of the facility. Pleasure to meet you!

We were thirteen at the time and I had no clue who he was. All I knew was the name Bear. Little did I know a decade later I would ask him to be the best man in my wedding.

When Joshua says that he used to be a pain in the ass, he means it. It was to the point that when four of us from our club soccer team committed to play at Vanderbilt, the other three of us met together trying to convince each other that we were a great fit as roommates. Honestly, no one wanted to be stuck with Bear, and not one of us lived with him during college.

People who don't know Joshua from back then have a hard time believing some of the stories. Those who do know him from back then have a hard time believing the transformation.

I'll be honest, it was even hard for me to believe in the beginning as I joined him in Train To Be CLUTCH. But I can attest to the proverbial blood sweat and tears that have gone into rewriting his story.

I was there when he was giving some of his first public speeches. No, not at Pepperdine, but back in public speaking 101 at Vanderbilt. What you see and experience today is a far cry from the friend I saw in a suit arguing his position on God-knows-what to a bunch of people who really didn't care. It wasn't polished. It wasn't pretty. And it was devoid of love. When he says that talent is a myth, he means it.

It was pretty eye opening to return to America, after living abroad for five years, and see how Joshua was transforming. I remember a night soon after I returned from Ireland very clearly. It was a night that changed my life and the legacy for future generations in my family. I could not shake the dream I believe God planted in my heart to pursue playing professional soccer. It made no sense in my mind. As I was telling Joshua about the dream I felt like a fool. (It had been over two years since I had been able to kick a ball due to an injury.)

There was no judgment. There was no life-altering workshop. Just a simple question: "Jamie, are you going to tell your kids to chase their dreams? If so, you better have chased yours."

For a guy who claims to no ask great questions, those few words radically rocked my world. That night set me onto a journey of learning what real hustle looks like. In all honesty, some of the things Joshua was encouraging me to do with my time, resources, and what to share in presentations made me feel very very uncomfortable. But if nothing else, Joshua gave me the courage to fail. Looking back, I never felt like I was being judged or sized up in any way. I never felt like I was a burden to the brand or a let down according to expectations. I was simply encouraged to have a growth mindset, experiment, and hustle.

I remember one day sitting on the couches here in Denver and I was letting out my frustration that I wasn't booking events and finding clients. Joshua didn't put it on me. He wrote out a commitment list that he encouraged me to focus on. It was simple: send @messages on Twitter, write an article each day, and keep reading. I stepped up my twitter presence and sure enough I began to see things change. By being faithful to the small stuff of providing value, I began work with a guy on the PGA Tour and a guy playing in the NFL.

Joshua didn't bitch and he didn't beg. He modeled hustle day by day and lovingly pointed me towards greatness: small things that seem like they make no difference at all while you are doing them, and doing them over and over.

If you choose to employ the strategies in this book over the next two to four years, things will not remain the same in your life.

A while back I found myself in a strange financial position. There were some things I would do differently if I could, but a few things were completely out of my control leaving me with no paid opportunity for over a month. To be honest, that felt like rock bottom for me. I poured out my heart in frustration, praise, and desperation to God. And nothing in my circumstances changed. But all of a sudden my training kicked into gear.

I got up and wrote out a "can do" list. At the top of the list was providing value on Twitter. So, I sent out thousands of videos to people, and some of those people started following me. I sent all of them video tweets thanking them for the follow and leaving a personal message of encouragement. At least one girl went on to get our book. And she loved it.

She told her dad that he had to read it. He loved it. He bought it for all of the executives in his organization. They loved it. Then I got a call from the leader of their sales team.

As I was getting prepared for the call, my training kicked in. "Jamie, this is not about getting a workshop booked. In fact, forget about a workshop. Provide value and ask great questions. If they ask about working, throw out the big number that you are afraid of saying. This is less about getting the opportunity and more about who you are becoming."

I surrendered the results.
I focused on what truly mattered.
I decided to provide value. No Matter What!

Three years ago when I started working with Joshua I was working on the outside staff at a golf course for $10 an hour. The two-day corporate training and workshop will pay me $10,000 plus travel expenses. Not only do I get compensated very well for my work today, but I also have the ability to spend lots of quality time raising my family and pursue my dreams.

I don't say that to brag. I tell that progression of events so that you understand this book is no joke, and it's not based on some theory. The model that Joshua has set for me is one that I dare not stray from. And if you choose to employ these strategies consistently, deliberately, and intentionally, then you will never be the same. Your life will never look the same.

I want you to understand that the stories and principles in this book are not made up and they are not theoretical. They are a blueprint for becoming the change you want to see in the world. As one who has embarked on this journey, I can honestly say that everything in here is simple, but little of it is easy.

My hope and prayer is that you will embrace the transformational journey of pursuing your personal greatness. Joshua's life story and the strategies in this book are the indisputable evidence of the transformational power of hustle.

I'm honored to have such a great role model and loving friend in my life. I pray that Joshua's life blesses you in the same way it has blessed me and my family.

With Love,

Jamie Gilbert

CHAPTER 1

Hustle

Hustle is the most important word ever. -Gary Vaynerchuk

Dreams are free.

Hustle is sold separately.

There has never been more opportunity in the world for those who are willing to hustle. The gatekeepers are all but gone, and it is those who are willing to hustle in the dark who will get to shine in the light.

Greatness isn't sexy, it is dirty hard hustle when no one is watching.

Greatness is 3% what everyone sees under the bright lights, and 97% your hustle in the dark, often when your dreams are so far off that they feel like fairy tales.

Never before has there been this kind of opportunity, but never before has there been this type of exposure either. No longer do you have a stranglehold on opportunity because of what zip code you were born into, your family line, your race, or because of who you know. The opportunities are greatest for those who are willing to hustle, because hustle itself does not discriminate. For those who want to mail it in, who want to coast after "making it," it is no longer safe. Never before have people had so many options, and if you don't stay hustling in the dark, you will be exposed in the light.

1

Never before have people had so much opportunity to not just make a living from doing the things they love, but to thrive. What has become consistently apparent once you get behind the scenes, is that those shining the brightest have been hustling in the dark the longest, typically while most of the world waits for their "big break."

They have been hustling while others have been hoping.
They have been hustling while others have been sleeping.
They have been hustling while others were dreaming.

They have been hustling from the beginning with few resources, and even fewer people who believed in them. But what they did have? Hustle, and lots of it.

Your dreams are waiting, but they require you to develop your hustle muscle in ways you never thought possible.

The process of becoming great is a long and painful road with no guarantee of success. The only guarantee is that you will have the chance to, over a long period of time and a long series of mistakes and hard failures, build yourself into the person you were born to be. And make no mistake about it, you were born to be great.

Your dreams are waiting, but they will require everything you have and more.

I believe in you.

"Under pressure you don't rise to the occasion, you sink to the level of your training. That's why we train so hard." –Heard from a Navy Seal

CHAPTER 2

Prison

I remember watching a really powerful stage drama one day about a group of people who were trapped inside a prison for many years. Eventually though, the prison doors were unlocked, the armed guards had abandoned their posts, but because of years of conditioning the prisoners refused to leave. A man came to visit them, pleading with them to go, but they chastised him and drove him away.

I think the same thing has happened in our culture today. All the rules have changed, and there is no reason to stay trapped in a job you hate, but for most people in our culture, that's really hard to believe.

It's hard to believe you could just walk away from prison and pursue your dreams and destiny. Most people would rather believe someone else is keeping them chained up, than accept the truth: the only one responsible for keeping us where we are, is us.

It's hard to believe the people who say, "You just need to adopt an abundance mindset." They sound a little crazy, I get it. But the truth is that we all already have an abundance mindset, but most people use this energy to create an abundance of excuses for not fulfilling their potential. Everyone has challenges. Some see them as an excuse, but the rare few choose to see them for what they really are; the forging ground for greatness.

When you've been stuck in prison for most of your life, it is hard to believe that the world is full of endless opportunities. But when people are turning things like worm poop into multi-million dollar businesses like TerraCycle, the truth is that there has never been an era of greater opportunity for anyone regardless of sex, race, zip code, and last name.

But the hard truth is this: no one can let you out of prison. You and you alone must choose to leave.

Most people never will. Most people will choose the three square meals per day and comfortable structure of a scheduled life, even if it is killing their potential. They prefer certainty over the wide-open Wild West-like culture of the internet, social media, and a constantly shifting landscape of new technologies.

I don't want prison though, and I hope you are courageous enough to break out with me, despite your conditioning and despite the stories that so many people have done their best to convince you are true.

"If someone insists they need to be in prison even though the door is unlocked, then I am not going to argue. They are free to stay in prison." — James Altucher

Google and watch the video "Trapped On An Escalator."

CHAPTER 3

Cut The Ropes

A man went on a family vacation to India and took his children to the zoo. They were having a blast, feeding all the different animals and enjoying the beautiful day. Finally, they worked their way to the zoo's prized animals: the elephants. The massive beasts roamed their paddock freely, with nothing but a single rope tied to a stick carried by one of the zookeepers to hold them back from the onlookers. Seeing this, the man's face went white, and he immediately grabbed his children and ran for his life in the opposite direction.

Seeing a zookeeper, he shouted at the man, "Are you insane?! You have two-ton beasts just roaming around here tied down only by a single rope?! They could snap that at any time and crush everything in their wake!"

The zookeeper nodded, but smiled. "Sir! Please calm down. I know that you're terrified and I know that the elephants are powerful beyond measure. But what you don't know is that when they are born, the very first thing we do is tie a rope around their leg. We tie the other end of the rope around a strong tree. When they are young, the rope is much stronger than them. They fight and fight and fight to break free from the rope, but eventually their will breaks first, and they come to believe that they can never break free from the rope. As they grow older, they do so with the belief that the rope has power over them. Even though they have massive potential and are amazingly powerful, they will never hurt us. Their belief about the rope holds them back."

The question we have to ask ourselves is:

What are the ropes in our life that have been holding us back?

What are the beliefs that we are clinging to that are keeping us stuck?

What are the beliefs that may have been true at one point in our life, but that are no longer true and are keeping us from achieving our greatest potential?

Whenever someone says something is impossible, ask the question, "Who says?"

You aren't smart enough. "Who says?"
You need another degree to be successful in this economy. "Who says?"
You are too old. "Who says?"
You are too young. "Who says?"
You don't have enough experience. "Who says?"
You can never play for that team or in that league. "Who says?"

Before Roger Banister broke the four-minute mile, people everywhere believed it was impossible to do so. But after he broke it, suddenly people all over the world began running sub-four-minute miles. It wasn't a change in training habits. It wasn't that a new generation of runners was suddenly faster. The only thing that changed was a simple belief. The rope had been cut. A false belief had been shed and now people were free to tap into their greatest potential.

These false beliefs are all around us, and many times we don't even know what they are until they are broken.

People once believed that your skin color determined whether or not you had the intellectual acumen to play quarterback or lead a team.

People once believed that your sex determined whether or not you could run a company or how much money you could make.

People have believed all sorts of crazy things that have held us back from

achieving our greatest potential.

So, we must continually ask, "Who says?"

I've recently noticed something: most often, it is the people who quit on their dreams (and who are usually miserable) who have the most to say about the people who don't.

Ignore the haters, and instead find stories of people who have overcome the odds. I had so many people tell me it was impossible. I had so many people tell me I was stupid for not writing my master's thesis at Duke. I know it sounds crazy, but I just kept studying Steve Jobs, Bill Gates, and Mark Zuckerburg, and I kept telling myself, "Joshua, if they can, why can't you?"

What beliefs do you need to let go of in order to fulfill your destiny?

CHAPTER 4

Build Wisely

Let me tell you a story about a carpenter from England named John. He had built hundreds of houses for his company over the last fifteen years, and his work was so good that the company became one of the premiere developers in the country. John worked extremely hard, putting in over-time nearly every day, and paying special attention to every detail on every project.

One day John decided he was going to retire. So he spoke with his boss about it, and they decided he would work one last week. His boss called him in the next morning and asked if he would build just one more house for a very special friend of his. Half-heartedly, John agreed and began work on the house.

Though he had built excellent houses in the past, this build was different. Many times in the past John had pushed through days and months where he struggled to find motivation, but he just didn't feel it on this proj-ect. Knowing this was his last go-round, John showed up each day with less focus than usual. He bought materials and supplies that were second rate. He delegated a lot of tasks without providing supervision. He only worked the hours he was "supposed to." He showed up every day with little joy and without the drive to be better than he was the day before.

Despite the lack of desire and motivation, the house was built on time and up to code, though far from his usual standard. Walking into the office, beaming ear to ear, John met with his boss to shake hands and say fare-well. As John walked towards the door, his boss called after him, "John, one last thing." As John turned to face him, his boss handed him a small box with

a ribbon around it. John opened the box and pulled out a set of shiny silver keys: keys to the house John just built. His boss smiled, "The house is yours, John. You deserve it."

Immediately, John's heart sank. If only he knew that he was building his own house, he would have done it all differently. He would have worked with the utmost passion and precision. He would have spent twice the amount of time and would have showed up every day with a clear focus on the job at hand, knowing that he was going to reap what he was sowing.

In everything you do, you are building your own house. Build wisely.

CHAPTER 5

Hiding From Police

When I asked myself what I would do if money didn't matter six months earlier, I didn't expect to find myself here. "Here" being alone, highly inebriated, in a field outside of Lamar, Missouri, population 9,876. Oh, and "here" also meant checking my phone to find a voicemail from the local police, telling me that I needed to turn myself in, as there was a felony warrant out for my arrest.

Yet there I was, twenty-three years old, having just finished up my classwork for a master's degree from Duke University, trying to sleep with all the big and small creatures who call the woods their home.

My father had taught me from a young age never to trust the police, and under no circumstance was I ever supposed to speak with them without a lawyer present. Strangely enough, at 4am in the morning, my lawyer was asleep about three hundred fifty miles from the field I had made my temporary home.

A few minutes after I dozed off, I jumped up out of my sleep to the sound of, "DA DOOM, DA DOOM, DA DOOM!"

I'd like to think that in that moment I was brave, but if I can be authentically vulnerable with you, I was the exact opposite. Like, peed-my-pants-a-little opposite. I had read recently that more people died from wild boar attacks than shark attacks, and in that moment I thought I was about to meet my maker while padding that stat.

Turns out it was not a wild boar; rather it was a Clydesdale horse, like from the Budweiser commercials. Apparently, a human sleeping in his domain was something he frowned upon, so I quickly made my way out of his field.

After searching for a while, I found an embankment on the side of the road, deep enough to be hidden from the view of any cops that might drive by. There, I was able take a brief nap while hoping the police didn't wake me up and drag me to jail.

In order to become the person I dreamed of becoming, it was obvious I had much to learn about the process of becoming great.

CHAPTER 6

You're Not In Kansas Anymore

Thankfully, I've come a long way since that night eight years ago in the field in Lamar, Missouri. Today, I've built the brand, Train to be CLUTCH, into a consulting power that many consider to be one of the best in the world. We created the first mental training apps in the world for soccer, basketball, and golf that are now in more than sixty countries. We have written many books, including the best-selling countercultural book Burn Your Goals, which is transforming the way many people train, parent, lead, coach, and live. (Go to www.t2bc.com/burnyourgoals to download a free copy.)

We work with people who are some of the best in the world at their craft, from the NBA, NFL, MLB, LPGA, PGA, MLS, Fortune 500, and almost every BCS school, as well as people in education, architecture, commercial photography, entertainment, and many other industries.

In less than five years, we've been able to build a million-dollar brand with only two people. I started it six years ago, and my best friend Jamie Gilbert joined me on the journey about three years after that.

I like to tell people that when I first started out I was probably one hundred fifty pounds mentally overweight, and that I still probably have at least fifty to go.

At the end of the day, I don't know why people listen to me. Anson Dorrance has won twenty-one national championships, and I have won zero. Many of the people I have influence over will end up in the Hall of Fame in their respective sports and professions. It sometimes amazes me that they listen to someone who often has very little experience in their given field.

Like I said, I can't tell you why people listen to me. But what I can tell you is what I have done, and more importantly what I haven't done, on my journey over the last few years toward building a million-dollar brand. Most importantly, I've written this book to share with you the lessons I've learned along the way.

I've been on this journey of learning how to hustle and fall in love with the process of becoming great for a while now, and most of the time I'm shocked to realize that much of what has been sold by "experts" is often destructive, and is often peddled by people who have no clue what it really takes.

This is my journey, and I hope it encourages, inspires, and possibly even teaches you a thing or two along the way. Most importantly, thank YOU, for taking the time to pick this book up and spend time with me. I truly consider it the most incredible privilege to be allowed to speak into your life, and it's one I do not take lightly.

Feel free to go over to t2bc.com/hustlebook to download the free accompanying resources to go along with the book.

Also, feel free to send me a tweet @joshuamedcalf to let me know your thoughts about the book as you go! (I personally respond to all of them!)

CHAPTER 7

The One Thing That Is Supposed To Change Everything

I struggled with girls growing up. I thought it was because my parents wouldn't buy me cool clothes that the boys who girls liked had.

Promise you won't laugh.

This delusion became so persistent, that I thought if I could just get a pair of Rock and Republic jeans, then girls would finally like me.

Okay, now you're laughing!

Obviously, I was super frustrated when I realized that just by putting on a pair of jeans, nothing really changed. I think we (myself included) have become infatuated with the idea of the silver-bullet fix, the "one thing that will change everything."

Maybe it is the seed money for your startup.
Maybe it is the introduction to the dream client.
Maybe it is a certain pair of shoes.
Maybe it is a certain type of camera.
Maybe it is a certain person for your team.

What I have come to realize, though, is that as soon as I get that thing that is supposed to change everything… not a lot changes. Seth Godin argues, "The only thing that changes, is that you realize you don't need that one thing as much as you thought you did."

I thought that after I knocked my workshop out of the park with the greatest dynasty in college sports, that people were going to beat down my door to work with me.

It was nine months before I booked my next major workshop.

I thought that after I gave a keynote in the corporate world, I would have so many opportunities in the corporate space that I wouldn't know what to do.

They loved it, but not much has changed.

It's comforting to believe in this "the-one-thing-I'm-missing-will-change-everything" theory, but you and I are much better off to just keep doing the dirty, hard work, every single day.

From what our clients tell me, the two things that have made the biggest difference for them, is simply to care about them as human beings, rather than dollar signs or production units, and to expediently respond to them. Sadly though, it's easier to believe you need a viral video, seed money, better resources, etc. than it is to do the dirty, hard work of actually caring and treating people well.

Focus on doing the little things in your hand really well, and less on the one thing that is supposed to change everything (which at the end of the day, might not even change anything).

"Greatness is a lot of small things done well day after day." — Ray Lewis

CHAPTER 8

YOU Inc.

"Would you hire yourself for a $500k job?"

It's often a sobering question I ask myself. It's also a question I ask the young people I get to influence.

I use to think no one took me seriously, but after taking a hard look at how I actually used my time, I realized I was the one who didn't take myself seriously. Once I took myself seriously, everyone else started to take me very seriously as well.

I'm not sure there has ever been a time where personal brands were more visible to the whole world. If you were hiring someone for an anchor role for ESPN wouldn't you go look at as many tweets, and other social media posts that person had put out over the last 5 years? I know I would.

Personal brands are no longer just about people like Kim K, and Gary Vee. Every single one of has a personal brand whether we realize it or not. Even the person serving as a janitor, and the person coaching a Pee-Wee league team.

The way you show up for class every day is a reflection of your personal brand.

The way you treat people is a reflection of your personal brand.

The way you show up for practice every day is a reflection of your personal brand.

What you choose to retweet and post on IG is a reflection of your personal brand.

Whether you choose to become a resource hub is a reflection of your personal brand.

Whether you choose to focus on the process or results is a reflection of your personal brand.

Whether you choose to be transformational or transactional today is a reflection of your personal brand.

The books you read, the books you don't read, what you wear, what you don't wear, how you dress, how you carry yourself, what you spend your money on, and how you consistently show up when you think no one is watching are all reflections of your personal brand.

Whether you realize it or not, every day people are buying or selling your stock. All the little choices you make about what time you get up, how you treat people, and how you serve all determine the stock price of YOU inc.

YOU inc. will only become more visible over the next ten years, and be sure that your work (or lack thereof) in the dark, will surely be revealed in the light.

Would an investment in YOU inc. be a wise one?

CHAPTER 9

Growing Up

"And so rock bottom became the solid foundation on which I rebuilt my life." – J.K. Rowling

Two weeks after my night in Missouri's "field of dreams", I started my drive to Los Angeles, California not knowing whether or not I had a felony arrest warrant out for me.

At the time, my uncle was a Captain in Oklahoma's Highway Patrol, and he helped calm my fears before I started my trip with this nugget of wisdom: "Joshua, if you get pulled over and you do have a felony arrest warrant out, you will have a gun pulled on you, cuffs slapped on you, and you will be thrown into the back of the patrol car until they get word on whether Missouri wants to extradite you."

Awesome! Well, at least I had that going for me.

A few days later I arrived in Los Angeles, thankfully without any of the aforementioned activities actually happening, but my challenges had just begun.

My mom says that we weren't poor growing up, but I haven't heard of many wealthy families who split 39-cent cheeseburgers and ice cream cones from McDonald's. I also haven't met very many wealthy kids who dreamed about getting a Happy Meal either, but maybe we weren't poor. Maybe my mom was just the most frugal person never to have lived through The Great Depression.

JOSHUA MEDCALF

My dad grew up in a trailer park and literally had to duct tape his trailer together. His own father left the family when he was still crawling around their trailer in diapers, and the only time I met him he was seemingly bunkmates with Frank from the TV show Shameless.

However, my dad was one of the most stubborn people I've ever met, and he eventually became an eye surgeon. It took him seven years of residency, because he kept getting rejected by his desired ophthalmology program, but after a few failed attempts they finally acquiesced and made a special spot for him (apparently, they realized he wasn't going to give up until they let him in.)

Based off of my father's relentless spirit and incredible drive, I went from dreaming about Happy Meals, to my family being able to afford to put me through Vanderbilt for college.

CHAPTER 10

Trust Your Gut

One thing I find so troubling about us as humans, is our tendency to keep those closest to us in a safe, comfortable box that stifles their potential. I call this box their "perception box," because any time you try to do anything outside of that box, they're quick to shut it down and kick you back into their safe little box with all the reasons why it is "impossible" and you aren't "qualified."

One of the most important lessons I've learned on my journey is that I needed to act outside that box if I was ever going to fulfill my God-given potential. That started with moving to a city where not one of the eighteen million people "knew" me.

When I asked myself what I would do if money didn't matter, the answer that shocked me and everyone in my life at the time, was that I would serve people.

Have you ever blurted something out when asked a question and then looked over your shoulder like that answer must have come from someone else?

Well, that was exactly how I felt.

Serve people?

My inner critic was saying, "Joshua, you're an a**hole that doesn't even like people! This has to be the stupidest idea ever!"

Yet when I got quiet, deep down in my gut I knew it was the only way forward for me. So to the shock and bewilderment of most of my friends and family, I skipped scholarships to law school, abandoned my hard-earned 3.8 GPA and master's thesis at Duke, and packed up my Tahoe with my TV and clothes to travel across the country and serve at a big homeless shelter in downtown Los Angeles.

It seemed crazy, but if Steve Jobs taught me anything, it was to trust your gut, and that crazy (but well-executed) ideas are what the world needs from you and I.

CHAPTER 11

Night Terror

The other confirmation I had arrived in the form of a night terror five months before the "field of dreams." I'd fallen in love with a girl whose family was incredibly wealthy, and that became the impetus for asking myself what I would do if money didn't matter.

A month after falling head over heels for this girl, it all came crashing down.

Walking with suitcases in tow to my best friend's apartment, I had tears flowing down my face. I knew sleep would be hard to come by that night.

Around nine p.m. I took some melatonin, and by ten I was fast asleep on my best friend's couch.

The next thing I knew, I felt someone pulling my hair like they were preparing to scalp me, and I looked over to find a guy staring right at me. His skeletal face was painted bone-white, and surrounded by a Jim-Carrey-esque shock of wild wavy hair.

"I'm going to KILL you!" he said.

Open your eyes! Open your eyes! Open your eyes, it's not real! (I kept trying to say to myself).

When I opened my eyes, I was comforted that Jim Carrey was gone, but frightened by the fact that my surroundings and the time of night were the exact same. I walked to the bathroom, and it was only then that I heard a man's footsteps walking out of the living room where I was just sleeping.

I don't know if it was a hallucination or a demon, but in that moment I knew that if I went to law school, it would be the death of me. I would wake up at fifty with a lot of toys, but I would wonder where my life went. I saw this happen to my dad when he was diagnosed with terminal cancer at forty-nine, and I was determined not to let it happen to me.

CHAPTER 12

Don't Wait Until You Have Terminal Cancer

My dad died at fifty years old. I was only twenty-two at the time, but I made a promise to myself, "Don't wait until you have terminal cancer to appreciate everything God has given you."

This night terror experience only confirmed what I already knew in my gut: that I desperately needed to move to L.A. and serve people, not go to law school.

The next day I flew home to Tulsa and Googled, "nonprofits in L.A." The L.A. Dream Center came up, and that was where I arrived, sight unseen, a few months later.

Upon arriving at the homeless shelter that I'd call home for six months, I had a strange peace about it. Tucked just outside of downtown Los Angeles, it was a dramatic shift from my last six years at Vanderbilt and Duke, but it felt like the perfect place to become the person I wanted to become.

When I arrived at "my" room, it was so crammed full of my new roommates' stuff that I decided to only bring in my TV and a few articles of clothing. My roommates were kind enough to clear off one of the bottom bunks that would be my new bed.

The room was filthy, and one of the guys had duct-taped cardboard boxes around the windows so zero sunlight would come through. He also liked to "clean" the room with chemicals, which didn't do much for the already-stale air quality (thanks to the windows being taped down). We shared a toilet and shower with our suitemates, and I somehow managed to never get any diseases from the mold and other unidentifiable fungus growing in the shower (however, I never stepped in without wearing sandals).

Across the hall from us lived a young married couple, and I ended up becoming close friends with the husband, who played basketball in college. Our assigned work was the food truck, which had great hours, so we were both happy.

My first day on the food truck, one of the guys told me about a weekly on-campus pickup basketball game on Wednesday nights, and it just so happened to be a Wednesday. Turned out it was an invite-only game, but for some reason the guy who ran it gave me a chance to play that first night.

From then on, he and I became incredibly close friends and we hooped together all over the city for the next few years. That night is one of my fondest memories of the homeless shelter. Sadly, it wouldn't be until many years later that I realized that the best friend I met that day would become one of the greatest inhibitors on my journey.

CHAPTER 13

I Didn't Ask...

Our responsibilities on the food truck were very simple. After breakfast we reported to the trucks, where pallets of food were waiting for us to distribute. Depending on the sizes of the groups we'd be delivering to around the city, each pallet would be loaded into the appropriate truck, and then we'd head out after lunch.

It didn't take long to realize that food truck duty wasn't exactly the "Harvard" of this place, but after we finished loading the truck in the morning we could shoot hoops or chill in our room, so I didn't mind it. Technically speaking, our "boss" told us we needed to go back to the office after we loaded the truck, but once I found out he just wanted us to sit there and do nothing until lunch, my hallmate and I stopped going back to the office after we loaded the trucks.

I fell in love with L.A. very quickly. I'll never forget sitting on the steps outside our dorm, telling my Mom on the phone that I was going to be there for a long time. I'd been there a grand total of three days.

But for a kid who'd been told he was different and difficult his whole life, L.A. seemed like a match made in heaven.

There was one thing that really bothered me about the food truck though. Every morning before we could load the trucks, we were supposed to wait on "the disciples" to come and wash and clean out the trucks from the previous deliveries.

The discipleship program was a very strict program, which contained folks on the path to recovery from severe drug and alcohol addiction. Many of them had spent a significant amount of time living on the street. All the disciples wore a certain type of black shirt, and they were forbidden from talking to anyone who wasn't in the discipleship program. The only exception was to talk about work-related issues.

Eventually, I got tired of this system, and I decided that my hallmate and I would take some initiative and start washing and cleaning the trucks on our own rather than waiting for the disciples to finish their morning program and do so.

Waiting really bothered me for two reasons. First, I struggle with patience. So waiting an extra thirty minutes for something I could do myself just seemed dumb. Second, I felt very uncomfortable with the perceived "you-are-beneath-us," and "we-are-too-good-to-clean-the-trucks" mentality that seemed to exist not too far beneath the surface of our fellow workers on the food truck.

My defiance of the status quo didn't go over too well with my fellow workers or my "boss." After it became enough of an issue with my co-workers, he pulled me aside one day and told me, "Look, this isn't the Ivy League or some fancy Fortune 500 company. This is a ministry, and we do things differently here."

I shrugged and said, "Great! Jesus washed the feet of his Disciples, so I think the least I can do is wash these trucks out for our disciples, instead of sitting around waiting for them to do it."

Apparently, he didn't appreciate my response, and he let me know, saying, "You aren't going to last long here."

That night, I was really struggling with his comment and I was left wondering whether I'd slipped back into my old ways and was "just being difficult."

27

I pulled out my Bible to a very familiar verse, Joshua 1:9. When I was nine years old God planted that verse in my heart, and it had always been my favorite verse. However, I had never read this translation.

"Have I not commanded you? Be strong and courageous, do not be afraid, for the Lord your God will be with you wherever you will go."
I had never heard or read that first part of the verse, "Have I not commanded you?" But that day, it felt as if God was speaking that question and verse directly to me, as if to remind me of my mission. He didn't ask. He commanded me, and my call was to be bold and courageous.

CHAPTER 14

Sucker Punch

I got into a few brawls growing up, but the majority of those were with people I knew I wanted to fight.

One of my roommates became more passive-aggressive over my first few months at the shelter, but I didn't think too much of it. He had taken to calling me "too cool," which I assumed showed his frustration with my lack of desire to befriend people I didn't want to spend time with. I knew some people were frustrated that the "cool kids" had taken a liking to me, but life goes on.

One day, I was briskly coming down the stairs in our building when I came across my roommate and another guy from our building. With a smile on my face, I playfully air jabbed at them both, nowhere close to touching them, said "what's up," and kept bounding down the stairs.

A few seconds later I sat on our couch, computer in lap, and flipped the TV on.

But the next thing I knew, my ear was ringing and I was completely disoriented. I popped off the couch as I tried to figure out what had happened, and why I couldn't hear out of my right ear.

When I turned around, my roommate was bouncing back and forth like a saber-toothed tiger, and his face was as red as a ripe tomato. He was yelling, and once my confusion faded a little bit, I started to realize he had just sucker-punched me in the ear. I told him that he had five seconds to apologize. He told me in very colorful language what I could do with my apology. So, I told him to pack his bags, because he was going home. It was the first time in my life that I had not retaliated when provoked, and it took everything inside of me not to. This guy deserved to get beat up, but something inside of me decided I was going to walk down the road less traveled.

Looking back, that was one of the most important lessons in learning to fall in love with the process of becoming great. If you sign up for greatness, a lot of garbage comes with it.

The true measure of a man is not how hard he fights back when provoked, but how much provoking he can endure, and still respond in love.

CHAPTER 15

Maybe I Should Give Up And Get A "Real" Job

Dealing with the repercussions of Mr. Sucker Punch was the first time in my life I really understood the strength required to "be the bigger person." The amount of grief I took from people for reporting the incident was immense. It was as if I was somehow the bad guy.

But then something really cool happened.

While meeting with the man in charge of the day-to-day operations of the campus, I was able to share my big idea with him. He loved it and set up a meeting for me with the founder of our non-profit organization.

When I finally met with the founder a few weeks later, he told me that my idea was "the best I've heard in fifteen years." I was over the moon! He asked me to put together a business plan, and then we could meet again in a month.

Wait a minute. A business plan?

I had no idea how to make a business plan, but I did have a person who might be able to help. My roommate from college was a guy named Brent Richard, and he was quickly excelling in the business and banking world, having recently become the youngest associate at Goldman Sachs.

I filled him in, and he agreed to help me put together the business plan.

After a lot of work, we had created something that we were both very proud of. It took about a month between our schedules to get it finished, but we both felt like it was really solid. Brent even offered to fly out and help me present it. I didn't think that was necessary, and I went into the meeting alone.

An hour later, I walked out frustrated and dejected. This was right around the height of the financial crisis in 2009. I had asked for a salary of $1,500 per month, and I was told they were cutting programs and couldn't afford to add on more expenses.

I had no clue at the time, but four years later I'd be able to command many times more than that amount to speak for 30-60 minutes.

At this point, I was incredibly frustrated, and even angry, with God. "Why did you give me this idea if no one is going to do anything with it?" In that moment, I felt abandoned.

I had yet to learn that true hustle is doing the best you can, with what you have, right where you are.

My bills were piling up.

My grandma was calling to check on me, because I was so late on my Tahoe payments that the repo man was calling for me.

Some days, I ate turkey out of the package, because it was all I could afford. In those days, I never knew what it was like to put more than twenty bucks worth of gas in my truck.

I couldn't help but wonder, was I crazy? Was this whole "L.A." thing worth it? Maybe I should just go home, try to get a "real" job, and give up on my dreams.

CHAPTER 16

Living In A Closet

If I had started out "difficult" in my job on the food truck, I had moved all the way over to "totally apathetic" by the end of my six-month internship.

I was given business cards, and became a "department head" of something that only existed in my head, but with no funding or idea of how to make it work. I felt stuck.

I had yet to learn that resources have a habit of following resourcefulness and faithfulness.

Then one day, I was riding to a conference in Arizona with one of my friends, and he asked me to share my big idea with the passenger, a guy named Matt. By the time I finished, Matt said he was going to talk to his dad, because their church was looking for someone like me to fill a role.

A few weeks later, I was invited down to meet the head pastor and leadership team. The head pastor happened to be Matt's dad. He showed me this huge gym that they hardly ever used, and asked if I was interested in starting my organization there. It seemed crazy to me, because they didn't have the infrastructure to house or school kids like I had pictured for my organization, but they filled my gas tank all the way up, and after the dog-eat-dog culture of the homeless shelter, I was very attracted to the church's more familial environment.

I left with no promises, but the head pastor was really excited about the possibilities.

Eventually, they invited me down again to meet the board, play golf, and discuss the logistics of bringing me on staff. When it was all said and done they offered me $1,500 a month to be their "sports director," with

the flexibility to start building my organization at the same time. I was given two housing options: I could live with a host family, or we could clean out a large closet in the gym and make that my home.

Naturally, I decided to move into the closet, with no windows, no air conditioning, a bathroom across the basketball court, and a shower that was across the court and down the stairs in the basement.

But honestly, that gym closet was a serious upgrade from the shelter.

Sure, it was a closet, and living there probably knocked years off my life, but it was my closet, and it meant that I had an opportunity to start building my organization.

Looking back, people tell me how amazing and ambitious I was, but in the moment it felt like anything but. Why? Because everyone loves stories of starting from the bottom, but not many people are actually willing to start there. You are often admired afterwards, but it can really suck while you're going through it. Remember though, no matter what obstacle you face, or how insurmountable it feels, one day that challenge will become a part of your story.

Have you ever heard a little kid say, "Tell me a statistic!"? Chances are you haven't. But I bet you've heard one say, "Tell me a story!" many times.

Make sure the life you are choosing today, is a story worth telling in the future.

"Make sure your willingness to sacrifice and how you use your 86,400 seconds are in direct proportion to the size of your dreams."

CHAPTER 17

The Day Everything Changed For Me

A few months after moving into the gym closet, my client list totaled three middle school boys. They didn't play at the professional, collegiate, or even high school level. They were just young kids who were passionate about basketball and football.

One day I was in the gym all by myself, and I got really frustrated that I only had three kids to train. I've probably always been a little optimistically delusional, and I truly believed that despite the fact that I was living in the closet of the gym, I could help any of the world's best in athletics.

I literally yelled out at God, "Why do I only have three kids? I could help Tiger Woods, LeBron James, or Michelle Wie. WHY DO I ONLY HAVE THREE PEOPLE?!"

It felt like He punched me in the chest as I heard, "Until you value those three little kids the same way you would, Tiger, LeBron, or Michelle, you will never work with a person of that caliber."

Not much has ever hit my heart in such a powerful way. My actions and beliefs drastically changed that afternoon in the gym. I did a complete one-eighty and have done my best to never look back since.

I started treating the kids I got to work with as if they were the most valuable and incredible people in the world. Since then, I've tried to never forget that, and to treat all the opportunities and relationships I've been given as if they are that dream client or that dream friendship.

Two years later, I was hired to do the biggest workshop I had done up to that point. I was supposed to start at 8:00 a.m. the next morning. I was with the head coach all day, so I didn't get to put the final touches on my presentation. All sorts of negative thoughts were going through my head.

"Are you really worth this much money?
"You don't belong here."
"You are a fraud."
"They are going to expose you."
"You should just go back home and get a real job."

To further complicate things, I got a text message from one of the people serving as my intern, "Hey, I really need to talk. Are you free?"

Are you kidding me? Right now? You want to talk right now? Don't you realize I have a big opportunity in front of me, and you are just a little one?

Then it hit me. If NBA All Star Chris Paul had texted me and asked to talk, would I have called him? Of course I would have, and I would have talked to him until 8 a.m. if that's what he needed. So, I needed to do the same thing for my intern.

I called her, and never mentioned what was going on in my life, or that she was prolonging my preparations for the next day. I did my best to be fully present, listen, and pour into her as best I could.

I got off the phone and less than two minutes later Jamie (my best friend) called me. At this point, Jamie was still playing professional soccer and I was serving as his mental coach. He wasn't a part of T2BC yet. Once again, those same thoughts ran through my head, and then I spent the next hour on the phone serving his needs without telling him about my circumstances.

When I got off the phone with Jamie it was past 1:00 a.m. and I still had to put the finishing touches on my presentation. I spent the next hour or so on my presentation, and then finally crawled into bed. The presentation and my time with the team the next day went really well, and I still work with their program to this day. But more importantly, I stuck to my principles.

It is so easy to look at what everyone else has -- their relationships, their clients, their resources, their opportunities -- and say, "Well, if I had that _____ then I would do _____." The harder but wiser thing to do, is to do the very best we can with what God has already placed in our hands. If we don't treat our Honda well, we probably aren't going to treat our Mercedes any differently. Sure, we might for a few months, but eventually, we will treat it the same way we did the Honda.

I call that day in the gym "The Day Everything Changed For Me" because ever since I started valuing and treating every person and opportunity as if it was the opportunity of my dreams, everything genuinely has changed in my life.

I love the way Seth Godin puts things into perspective in "The Interim Strategy."

"We say we want to treat people fairly, build an institution that will contribute to the culture and embrace diversity. We say we want to do things right the first time, treat people as we would like to be treated and build something that matters.

But first... first we say we have to make our company work.

We say we intend to hire and train great people, but in the interim, we'll have to settle for cheap and available. We say we'd like to give back, but of course, in the interim, first we have to get...

This interim strategy, the notion that ideals and principles are for later, but right now, all the focus and resources have to be put into the emergency of getting successful—it doesn't work.

It doesn't work because it's always the interim. It never seems like the right time to stop doing what worked and start doing what we said was important.

The first six hires you make are more important than hires 100 through 105. The first difficult ethical decision you make is more important than the one you make once you've (apparently) sions and playing the short-term game?

All the great organizations I can think of started as great organizations. Tiny, perhaps, but great.

Today, I get to work with people who have a slightly higher public profile, but if Erik Sheets (my first kid from the gym) texts me, he knows he can get ahold of me just like anyone else I work with. And when he wants to train, I always make the time.

I don't know where you are at in life, or how trivial your work seems at times, but I promise everything in your life will change if you will value your clients and everything you put your hand to as if it was the opportunity of your dreams. made it. The difficult conversation you have tomorrow is far more important than the one you might have to have a few years from now.

Exactly how successful do we have to get before we stop cutting corners, making selfish deci-

I don't know where you are at in life, or how trivial your work seems at times, but I promise everything in your life will change if you will value your clients and everything you put your hand to as if it was the opportunity of your dreams.

CHAPTER 18

Fast Forward

Fast-forward five years. I wrote my first book, Burn Your Goals, with Jamie Gilbert, and a person who mentors some of the most high-profile people in sports really fell in love with the book. On numerous occasions, he would call me and ask for advice on what to share with this guy who, for anonymity's sake, we'll call "Babe Ruth."

This went on for seven or eight months: he would call me every now and then, asking what I would tell someone in this situation or with that going on. Truthfully, I was thrilled to be able to share advice with him. Eventually I started to realize that many of the videos, articles, and mp3's I sent to him weren't being opened, let alone passed along. Then one day, he called to admit that he hadn't looked at much of what I sent, but he was finally at a place where he was ready to dig deeper into our tools. He asked if I would send some of our stuff over to him once again.

"No problem," I told him, but then he asked me to do one more thing before I sent anything. He asked if I would pray to see if the Holy Spirit put anything on my heart specifically for "Babe Ruth."

I didn't think I needed to pray about it, but on numerous occasions this guy had told me that while praying, God had put me on his heart for "Babe Ruth," so I decided it couldn't hurt to pray.

I was less than thrilled about what God put on my heart when I prayed. It felt like I was being asked to go kick a bear cub in front of the mama bear. But, reminded of that phrase "Have I not commanded you?" I reluctantly started typing up what I felt the Holy Spirit had put on my heart.

39

Basically, what I felt the Holy Spirit said was, "You need to treat 'Babe Ruth' like Eric Sheets." You see, when I first started working with Eric he called me "Mr. Pain." The workouts I would put him through were extremely challenging, and they'd often leave him hating me. He always knew that he could leave any time he wanted, but he rarely took the easy way out.

It wasn't until a couple years into our training, that Eric finally understood the value of our tough training sessions. He realized the truth behind the Navy Seals quote, "Under pressure you do not rise to the occasion. Rather, you sink to the level of your training." And nowhere before or since -- no team practice, camp, or anywhere else -- did he get trained harder than he did with me.

He learned how to fall in love with the process of becoming great in our training sessions, and it was a 'no excuses' environment. When we worked out, the question I constantly peppered him with was, "Do you want to get better or do you want to go home?" And so, he was trained like he played Division I sports from the time he was eleven years old.

What hit me in the heart when I was praying that day was that because of who "Babe Ruth" was, I was trying to make things easier and make excuses for him. I was allowing his mentor to make excuses for him, instead of doing what I had always done, just ask the simple question, "Do you want to get better or do you want to go home?"

That is exactly what I did, though I knew it might come at the potential cost of losing out on working with him forever.

I shared with his mentor that I would love to help "Babe Ruth" but that he would have to fully commit to training and it would cost a lot of time and energy. It wouldn't be convenient and it wouldn't be easy. It would be, as Ben Hogan said about greatness, "dirty, hard work."

That was months ago, and I haven't heard from him since.

Was it frustrating? Absolutely. But like Seth Godin taught me, "Everyone is not your customer."

Maybe I will work with "Babe Ruth" one day, maybe I won't. But my responsibility is to treat every Eric Sheets like "Babe Ruth" and every "Babe Ruth" like Eric Sheets. If I don't, then I am only setting them up for failure. Our brand is called Train to be Clutch for a reason. It's simple, but simple doesn't mean "easy" "quick" or "convenient."

CHAPTER 19

"What Do You Do With All Your Time?"

"Joshua, what do you do with all your time?" Russ asked me the day we first met.

It was such a simple question, but looking back it completely changed the trajectory of my life. I had just quit my job, moved out of the closet of the gym and into an apartment with my mom, and I was focusing on building my non-profit organization.

In the moment, I got up on my high horse and pontificated about all the things I did with my time. I told him about the non-profit I started and how I trained kids in the toughest housing project in the country. I told him about the humanitarian events that my friend and I would plan and run. I told him that I need a social life, right?

He seemed to have bought it, but hard questions always trump easy answers, and that question haunted me.

Time is the only resource that is the same for everyone regardless of how much money you make, your race, or where you live. We all only get 86,400 seconds per day.

John Wooden said, "The softest pillow is a clear conscience." Well, my soft pillow quickly began to feel like a crusty hard rock at night.

I knew I had massive dreams, and how I used my time (hustle) was not in direct proportion to the size of my dreams.

I started cutting a lot of stuff out of my life and drastically changed what I did with my time. I was guilty, as many of us are, of running towards all the stuff that was keeping me from my dreams: friends, chilling, Facebook, TV, staying busy, parties, and many other time wasters. For the first time in my life the size of my hustle started to match the size of my dreams.

For six months, I studied like a student in medical school, reading for up to fifteen hours a day. Most of my friends and family told me I was crazy. I had to block out a lot of noise from outside influences. When you are climbing out of a bucket full of crabs, there will be many people who try to pull you back down to their level.

Today, I get to coach and mentor a lot of amazing people, but it wasn't always like this. There was a time when no one was asking me to mentor them, but back then my circle needed a serious upgrade.

Certain people had to go. They were negatively influencing my decisions, and it was my responsibility to change how I spent my time and with whom I spent it.

The majority of my circle at that time came from spending time with Abraham Lincoln, Steve Jobs, Jesus, MLK, and other people whose lives I wanted to model. You may not have physical access to the ideal people for your circle yet, but we all have access to books, mp3's, and videos where we can bring the greats into our circle.

You don't have to be a jerk or tell the people of your current circle that they have been negatively influencing you. You can treat them very well, but still consciously choose to spend much less time around them.

According to a study done by a Harvard professor and published by the New England Journal of Medicine in 2007, you are 57% more likely to become obese if a person close to you becomes obese.

It's never easy to spend less time with people you've been around for a-while, but at some point you have to remember that you are the one who is building your own house. Most people have no clue how to hustle.

Your choice creates your challenge. You never know, they might start following you when they see things in your life starting to change for the better. Maybe they will call you names and treat you poorly, but either way, how they treat you is outside of your control.

After six months of spending the majority of my time reading and study-ing, I found myself in an elevator with Anson Dorrance. Anson serves as the Head Coach of the University of North Carolina Women's Soccer program. We got off the elevator, and while everyone else turned right, Anson and I turned left.

I asked him, "Who works with your girls on mental training?"

He said, "I do. I can read and write!"

Touché! If I had won twenty out of a total of thirty national champion-ships ever held in my sport, I would probably be very confident in my work as well.

So, I asked if he knew who Barbara Fredrickson was, and he replied, "I do not. Why should I?"

I spouted off my response at the pace of an auctioneer.

"Her research on positivity shows that if your positivity ratio is around 1 to 1 that forecasts clinical depression. If your positivity ratio is around 2 to 1 that forecasts languishing in life. But if your positivity ratio is over 3 to 1 it hits this funny tipping point and it starts to forecast flourishing, regardless of how you define 'flourishing.' It also impacts individuals and teams in a similar way. Oh, and she teaches at a little school you might be familiar with, the University of North Carolina at Chapel Hill."

A huge smile spread slowly across his face, and he stopped in his tracks.

"Can you write that down for me? You might have just made my trip here worthwhile."

Three months later, he invited me out to work with his program as only the second outsider ever to work with the UNC Women's Soccer program on mental training.

For a long time, I was really frustrated because I felt like nobody took me seriously. Now looking back, I realize the real problem was that I didn't take myself seriously. When I started taking myself seriously, I started hustling like my dreams depended on it, and most people started to take me very seriously as a byproduct.

We have control over how we use our time (hustle), but we don't have control over our goals. We know it is counter-cultural and potentially crazy to let go of goals. It goes against everything most parents, mentors, self-help books and expensive special consultants implore us to do. That is why Jamie and I wrote the book, Burn Your Goals. What it really comes down to is this...

Everyone wants to be great, until it's time to do what greatness requires.

Anyone can set a big sexy audacious goal, but very few people are willing to commit to focusing 100% of their energy on the things they have complete control over in life, like falling in love with the process of becoming great, and doing the boring work with excellence.

If you feel stuck, or like you haven't made it to the level you know you're capable of achieving, take a hard look at who is in your circle and how you use your time.

If you are frustrated with the things that keep happening in your life, take a hard look at those with whom you are spending your time. If you continually find yourself at the wrong place at the wrong time, take a hard look at your circle.

If you want to achieve your greatest potential, you must surround yourself with people who love you deeply, believe in you, and encourage you, but who are also willing to challenge you to become the best you can be by modeling greatness for you.

My encouragement to you would be to actually track how you use your time each day for the next week. Most people are shocked at how they actually use their 86,400 seconds.

CHAPTER 20

Do You Have The Mindset Of A Lion Or A Zebra?

There is an old African proverb that goes like this…..

Every morning the lion wakes up and it knows it has to be faster than the zebra if it wants to eat. Every morning the zebra wakes up and it knows it has to be faster than the lion if it wants to survive.

Regardless of a whether you are a lion or a zebra you have to get up ready to run if you want to survive.

One of my many problems growing up, was that I had a zebra mentality. But I wasn't trying to be faster than the lion, I was only trying to be faster than the slowest zebra. I was focused on doing just enough to get by, just enough to get a passing grade, just enough to not get yelled at by my coach, just enough to keep my job.

Much like the zebra I looked at every day like a test that was pass or fail, instead of seeing everything as an opportunity. An opportunity to learn and grow, an opportunity to get better, an opportunity to build my own house, an opportunity to invest in those around me.

The zebra can't seek out opportunities because they are always in survival mode, and on the lookout for danger. This was me, I was always trying to avoid danger, rather than seeking out opportunities. It was pretty much what everyone else around me did as well.

A wise man once told me, the lion and the zebra are both inside of you, and every single day you make a choice between which one you are going to feed and develop.

When you start to really hustle, you are going to face negativity and discouragement from everywhere, and often from very well-meaning people that are close to you. If you want a shot a making your dreams come true you must be deliberate, consistent, and persistent when it comes to feeding the Lion inside of you and starving the Zebra.

Will you seek out the opportunities all around you? Will you constantly be looking for 10 minutes here and 15 minutes there, where you are able to read a good book, invest in those around you, and make sure you are maximizing your 86,400 seconds per day? Because those opportunities are everywhere around us, but for most of us it takes a rewiring of our brain to see them and take advantage of them.

If I can be honest with you, most people are just trying to be a little bit faster than the slowest zebra. They are focused on avoiding danger and merely surviving.

- Surviving the budget cuts.
- Surviving the recession.
- Surviving the practice.
- Surviving the relationship.
- Surviving the layoffs.

I don't know about you, but I made up my mind a long time ago that I'm not interested in surviving. I want to thrive, not just merely survive. I want to become the type of person who is constantly hunting for opportunities everywhere I go. The sad thing is that society is always going to push you towards having the mindset of a zebra. From the time you are 5 years old they tell you:

- Get in line
- Shut up
- Sit down
- Don't stand out
- Color inside the lines
- Do what you are told
- Never question authority
- Live for the weekend
- Personal development is stupid
- Do just enough to get by
- Everything is a test, and if you don't do well you won't get to do your dream.

My life changed when I made the switch from a zebra mindset to that of a lion. It was extremely hard in the beginning, and it took a long time to break a lot of the habits that had been engrained in me since I was in elementary school, but eventually I started to see opportunities where other people only saw problems. I started to see and recognize diamonds in their rough state that others thought were old rocks.

You might be thinking, "Joshua, every day I wake up ready to run, and I work incredibly hard!"

Even if you are different than me, and you are trying to be the fastest zebra you can be, you are still going to hit a ceiling. If we learned anything from the last decade it is that there is no such thing as a "safe job" or "safe investment" anymore. Just because you are focused on the being the fastest zebra, you are still in survival mode.

The implications for your health alone are worth making the shift, because if you are constantly in survival mode you are operating out of 'fight or flight,' which has serious consequences on your immune system and overall levels of health. For the sake of your potential, your dreams, your health, and your family, you must start developing the mindset of a lion, and get out of survival mode.

You can't achieve billion dollar dreams with a minimum wage mindset.

Everyday you have a choice over who you will become. Are you going to feed the zebra inside of you, and believe all the lies?

- You aren't smart enough
- You aren't talented enough
- You are too old
- You are too young
- You aren't pretty enough
- You aren't good enough
- You don't have the resources
- You don't have the right pedigree
- This is impossible

Are you going to believe all those lies, and all the people who want you to believe them??

OR

Are you going to feed the lion, and believe the truth inside of you? That still, soft voice that says:

- You are more than a conqueror
- You were perfectly and meticulously created for a purpose
- You are created for incredible things
- You have a future and a hope
- You have greatness inside of you

It is going to be hard.
It is going to be tough.
You are going to have to change the way you see the world.
You are going to have to change how you spend your time.
You are going to have to change who is in your circle.
You are going to have to change what you habitually do.

Will you unearth and develop the greatness inside of you?
Are you going to feed the lion, or the zebra?

CHAPTER 21

Self-Directed Trumps Rote Learning

I've noticed something ironic in the world. Often it seems like the thing most people tell you is a weakness in your life, eventually becomes your greatest strength.

The tough part is that very few people are willing to hustle and persevere long enough to reach the tipping point.

When I first started out, I was repeatedly told that my lack of academic credentials was going to always hold me back. What I've now realized is that my lack of academic credentials has allowed me to become so much greater than I ever would have become with them. I went on a self-directed journey that was fascinating and exhilarating. I wasn't studying what someone told me to study just to pass a test. I was studying and reading everything that I found interesting and intriguing.

When you don't have a Master's or a PhD to fall back on, you better be well prepared when you get an opportunity to impact people's lives. Otherwise, you won't get many more opportunities!

Look at these two circles. Imagine that the dots in each of these circles represent people.

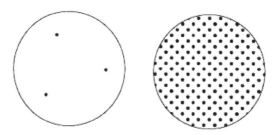

How replaceable are any of the people in the circle on the left?

Virtually impossible, right?

Now, how about the circle on the right? How replaceable are each of those people?

Highly replaceable, right?

If you're going through a degree program and learning what tens of thousands of other people are learning and studying, then even if you are the very best, you're still highly replaceable. When you go on a self-directed journey, you're learning things and developing skills that make you highly irreplaceable. Even if you aren't the best, it's still very hard to replace you.

Obviously, there is absolutely nothing wrong with going to school and getting specialized degrees, but if you want to become highly irreplaceable you better start to take control of your personal growth and education.

My formal education has been helpful, but I wish someone would've taught me all the principles in this book about true hustle when I was much younger. It took a long time before I moved from the right circle to the left circle, and I don't plan on ever going back.

CHAPTER 22

Dream BIG, Think Small

Let me share something you have hopefully figured out by now: ideas by themselves are worthless.

Apple started in a garage.
Subway started in a dorm room.
Nike started with Phil Knight selling shoes out of his trunk.
Facebook started in a dorm room.
J.K. Rowling wrote Harry Potter living on welfare after being abandoned by her husband with their infant daughter.
I built the first mental training apps in the world for soccer, basketball, and golf living with my mom, sleeping next to my little brother.

The land of faithfulness and execution of the small stuff is where money and opportunities live.

Everyone has great ideas, but what the success or failure of those ideas depends upon is not funding. Instead, it is dependent upon your willingness to sacrifice, hustle and do the hard work to turn that idea into a reality.

I'm so thankful I didn't get funding for my first idea at the homeless shelter. I wasn't even close to prepared for it. I had no clue what to do. I know that now, but back then I had no clue that I didn't know it. I would have told you I knew exactly what to do and that it would've been great. I was young, naïve, and arrogant.

Too many people get themselves in trouble because they create expenses rather than cash flow, and all they think they need is to raise $10 million in the next round of funding.

Here is my best advice:
Stop trying to pitch your idea.
Start building a minimum viable product and figuring out whether people actually want your product or service.

In my experience, most of the coolest businesses come from people who are willing to do the dirty, hard work to solve some personal or communal challenge that affects them. The money comes as a byproduct of their faithfulness to the small stuff.

The cool opportunities will come, but you have to remain faithful to the little stuff. One of my childhood friends is married to Blake Griffin's brother, and I know I could help Blake. But I have never said a word to her or Taylor about it.

I also know the Vice President of the Clippers and I'm great friends with one of the coaches on their staff, but I don't ever say anything.

Maybe I will work with Blake or the Clippers organization one day, maybe I won't.

Maybe Facebook, Google, Twitter, Nike, Apple, or any other big company or person would benefit greatly from your product or service. Maybe you would be the perfect partnership for them, but maybe you wouldn't.

A few weeks ago, I had the privilege of hearing Gary Vaynerchuck speak. He has been one of my business mentors from afar over the last few years. During Q&A he was asked, "When and how is best to pitch you, or people like you?"

His response? "You won't listen, because you won't have the patience. But my answer is, don't pitch us."

He went on to say that people like him will find you or your service, they don't need you to find them.

My challenge to you is to be so incredibly faithful with your small opportunities that that company or person comes knocking on your door. I based the business plan for my non-profit on IMG Academy. Seven years later, IMG Academy started knocking on my door asking if I was interested in heading up their Mental Conditioning and Leadership department, and I was at a place where I was able to politely turn them down.

I can promise you this, that when you have truly fallen in love with the process of becoming great, then you will have people that you never dreamed you'd work with knocking on your door.

Greatness NEVER goes on sale, and excellence sells itself.

Show is MUCH greater than tell.

What is the smallest version of your dream that you can be faithful with today, doing the best you can with what you have, right where you are at?

"I'm convinced that about half of what separates the successful entrepreneurs from the non-successful ones is pure perseverance." — Steve Jobs

CHAPTER 23

Stop Playing Small

"Think you are too small to make a difference? Try sleeping with a mosquito." – Dalai Lama

What if Steve believed he had nothing to offer the world, or what if he gave up after Apple kicked him out?

What if Mark quit after Wall Street said he wasn't capable of running Facebook?

What if Jack had listened to everyone who said Twitter was the stupidest thing ever?

What if Mother Theresa wouldn't have been faithful with the mission God put in her heart?

What if Nelson Mandela had believed all the people who said he was a "terrorist"?

And what about all the people we've never heard of who poured into all the people mentioned above, and encouraged them to be bold and courageous?

We probably won't create the next Apple, Facebook, or Twitter. We probably won't become the next Mother Theresa, Nelson Mandela, or Dalai Lama, but the world still needs us to solve that problem, build that tool, or encourage that one person on your mind.

Stop asking, "Who am I to do it?" and start asking, "Why not?!"

Stop playing small. The world needs you to become the best version of yourself.

Be faithful with small, treasure small, but stop thinking you are too small to make a difference.

In 2012 Bronnie Ware published a book, The Top Five Regrets of the Dying. The number one regret was, "I wish I'd had the courage to live a life true to myself, and not the life others expected of me."

CHAPTER 24

There Is Always A Back Door

Most people told me it was impossible to do what I wanted to do without the academic credentials. Now, people ask how we did it.

Most people think something is impossible until it's done.

Remember, the idea that the world was flat was around for a long time, and I believe people were actually killed for claiming otherwise. Imagine talking about building an airplane back then?

Let me explain something to you. The status quo has a vested interest in keeping you from changing things, even if it would make things better. Better for most people, rarely means better for the people in power.

Do you know how much money companies spend on lobbying efforts to keep polluting us with food that is killing us? Do you know how much money they spend to make sure the government continues to subsidize these foods, instead of organic foods, so that the prices of food that kills continues to be cheaper than food that is good for us?

Very well-meaning people told me for a very long time that I needed a sport psychology degree to do what I wanted to do at the level at which I wanted to do it. Thankfully, I didn't listen. There is nothing wrong with getting a degree, but for some people that isn't the most beneficial path for them or the world.

I'm so grateful that Jobs, Zuckerburg, and Gates all dropped out of school.

I'm so glad I didn't write my master's thesis at Duke, because it would have made things so much easier for me when I was starting out, and I needed to go up the rough side of the mountain to become everything I was capable of becoming. If I had written that thesis, there is very little chance you'd be reading this today, and that I would have even a tenth of the influence and opportunities I have today.

I burned all my ships, and I had nowhere to go but forward. There was no back up plan. I needed to be molded, shaped, and forged in the dark. The dark is where I grow the most. When someone tells you something is impossible, always remember that they might have a vested interest in keeping the status quo unchanged. Always ask the question, "Who says?" It won't necessarily earn you many friends in leadership, but it is a powerful question for your potential.

Most importantly, remember what Jamie Gilbert always tells me, "There is always a back door."

You can choose yourself.
You can just do it.
You can build the road.
You can build the back door.
The world has changed.
Sop complaining that you haven't been chosen.
Choose a mission.
Choose yourself.
Start hustling.

And always be bold and courageous enough to become so great they can't ignore you!

CHAPTER 25

The Necessity Of "Lack"

I hate to admit it, but I don't think you would be reading this if I had gotten a comfortable job right out of college. I don't think I would have ever truly learned how to hustle for real had I not been turned down by Enterprise Rent-A-Car, Target, and Starbucks for entry-level jobs. I don't think I would have become even close to the person I am today if I had had it easier in life.

Our society is obsessed with abundance, but the lack of it often stretches people to levels of intellectual creativity and resourcefulness others have never tapped into.

It's rare to find a person fed with a golden spoon who ends up transforming the world. Rarely are they the type of people anyone else strives to become.

What if having less initial resources, success, and opportunity was actually the foundational building block of personal greatness?

It sure seems that way.

This is why I don't understand people whose greatest dream is for their kids to "want for nothing." Our fear of failure for the next generation is creating an entire generation primed for mediocrity at best, and crippled by normal setbacks at worst (in comparison to living out their greatest potential).

Experiencing repeated failure and lack of resources is part of the formula for bringing out the deepest creativity, resourcefulness, and persistence needed to reach personal greatness. Lack produces certain things comfortability never will.

Be careful. "Success" and an abundance of resources can be the greatest obstacles to you becoming everything you can be.

I'm not scared of losing everything, because I know how to build it right back up again. I'm not scared of failing, because I've lived in a homeless shelter. I'm not scared of bankruptcy, because I've been broke.

Don't worry about a lack of resources. Instead, focus on using whatever you do have to hustle after what really matters: falling in love with the process of becoming great.

"Hardships often prepare ordinary people for an extraordinary destiny."
–C.S. Lewis

CHAPTER 26

The Illusion Of $

It seemed money was always the thing my parents were arguing about.

The question, "What would I do if money didn't matter?" has become such a liberating litmus test for my life. I sometimes don't operate by this principle, but I've found things usually work much better when I do. There have been many times where I have turned down very lucrative opportunities that I would have only done for the money, and there have been plenty of times where I have not been compensated like I should, but I still chose to do them anyway.

One of the most interesting realizations I've come to on my journey of falling in love with the process of becoming great is that money is an illusion.

Money (currency) is only as good as the thing that backs it, and that is why one dollar today could be worth fifty cents tomorrow, or it could be worth three dollars tomorrow.
Some time ago, the United States moved away from the gold standard. The gold standard meant that for every dollar of currency in circulation there had to be actual gold in the treasury that backed the value of that currency.

Today, Fort Knox is supposed to be home to a good portion of the gold the United States owns. But, and this is a really big but, no one in the general public can actually find out if the gold is even there, or if so, how much there actually is.

We literally don't know if there is any actual resource backing our currency.

If you need further proof that money is an illusion, just remember that when the government needs more money, they literally just print it. Or for further proof, just ask people who had a lot of money in the stock market in 2008-2009 about the illusion of money. Overnight, many people lost 20-50% of their life savings.

I use the word "illusion" purposefully here. I'm not saying that money doesn't exist, or that a person doesn't need some of this illusion to function within the confines of our current society. What I am saying is that when you start to understand that money is an illusion, it can make it easier to stop chasing it. It can make it easier to understand how some people make money grow on trees, while others can't seem to find it anywhere, and still others break their backs for so little of it.

Much like trying to squeeze water in your hands, the harder you squeeze, the more water you lose. I realized at some point in my career that money was never the real problem. I think it was Dale Carnegie who said, "There is the real problem, and then there is the problem people will tell you."

What I have found is that money is never the real issue for why someone, some business, or some entity cannot work with us or have us out to speak. The real reason is value.

Look at impoverished communities around this country, and what you will always find is that people will sacrifice to buy what they value. In the projects, you often see people wearing very expensive Air Jordans. In middle class homes, you often see Starbucks and nice cars in driveways.

I remember when I was living in the closet of the gym and I was living off about two hundred fifty to three hundred dollars per week. One day, I found a hoodie that I loved, but it cost two hundred fifty dollars.

I bought it.

I was willing to eat peanut butter and honey sandwiches and not drive my truck all week so I could barely have enough money to proudly wear that hoodie.

Why? Because I valued it.

We pay for what we value, and we sacrifice what we don't. Simple enough. When people say they can't afford to bring us out to speak or go through our mentorship program, what they're really saying is, "I don't value what you bring to the table at the same level you do."

Take a look at your life. What are you unwilling to sacrifice? What do you always make sure you have money for?

The flip side of the equation is that we often don't value what we don't pay for. When I work with a person who makes $100k a year, and another person who makes two million a year, who do you think values our time together more? In my experience it is the person who makes $100k a year, because it costs him more for us to work together.

Ever notice that a kid who is working two jobs to pay his way through college doesn't miss as many classes as the kid whose parents are paying the bill? When it costs me something, then I am much more likely to value it.

I wore that hoodie almost every day for two years, because I valued it.

Start to understand that money is an illusion, that we pay for what we value and we value what we pay for, and you will start to unshackle yourself from the money illusion that most people spend their whole lives trapped inside.

CHAPTER 27

Knocked Out

On New Year's Eve of 2012 I went down to San Diego to bring in 2013 with some of my friends from college. I had been serving as the director of mental training for UCLA women's basketball since September of that year.

The night before NYE I had fallen back into some old patterns and got myself into not one, but two scuffles with random guys at the hotel. It is so easy to fall back into bad habits, especially when changes in your life are more fresh.

The second scuffle then ended with my friends all getting in a big fight, and in all stemmed from my behavior. The next morning amidst the broken table from the friends fight we realized we not only lost the table, but one of our friends had packed his stuff and gone home. I felt so bad. Here I was this guy who supposedly helps all these people, and I'm looking no different then I was in college. I took a nap that afternoon, and promised myself and everyone else that I was going to do better.

At the end of the night of NYE, all the venues at the Hard Rock Hotel let out at the same time and there were a lot of people who were all trying to get on the hotel elevators. Our group of fifteen or so people worked our way towards the elevator and half of our group got on the elevator while

the other half of us did not. I had done so well, until all of sudden I heard someone say the most derogatory racist phrase you can say. It was so horrific; I couldn't believe it had been said. I must have been mistaken.

Then I surveyed the crowd around me and there were only two African American people in the general vicinity, and both of them were my friends. Sure enough, one of them was pulling the other one away from where I thought I heard the person make the racist comment. So, I moved closer to where I thought it came from.

Sure enough, I heard the person say it again, "F that N-word!" and this time I was looking right at him. Now, I'm not sure exactly what I said, but it was probably something along these lines, "Are you FREAKING kidding me?!" I might have used a different word or two in the heat of the moment, but who can be sure?!

Apparently, he wasn't kidding.

Very quickly he jabbed me in the nose. Now, right as I was saying what I said to him I looked over his shoulder at the group of guys surrounding him. There were about four or five guys that would have made an NFL Defensive line look small. They had to have averaged 6'6" 270lbs.

I could have taken the first jab from the little guy. He was probably in the ball park of 5'10" 155lbs, no big deal. But, while I was stunned from the quick first jab, one of the much larger guys throws a superman punch that knocked me out for plus or minus 15 seconds. Thankfully it was one of the smaller guys who threw the punch. He was only about 6'4" 240 lbs!!!

Even though I blacked out from the punch, I didn't actually get knocked off my feet. I like to tell people that's because I played division 1 sports, but it was more likely because there were a lot of people around and I just pin-balled off of them.

As I came to, I was very confused at the liquid that was flowing all over my face like an ice cream cone on a hot summer day. When I saw a security guard with a shirt trying to stop the bleeding, I realized it was actually my blood everywhere. A couple hours later after the bleeding stopped and I was able to take a shower, two of my friends took me to the hospital. As I am lying in the hospital bed I looked over at them and said, "I'm really glad that this happened! I believe it was in my best interest and an opportunity for me to learn and grow." Imagine the looks on their faces and what was going through their mind. "Are you serious?! We knew you had a couple screws loose, but we brought you to the wrong hospital. That guy must have pushed you over the edge, you are officially crazy. How in the world could this be in your BEST interest?!"

Believe me. I had many other thoughts going through my head. "You are a fraud! You are a fake! You can't help people! You need to resign. You haven't made any changes. You are the same stupid person who can't help but find trouble wherever you go! Once people find out about this you are going to need to find a new career!

However, I had been studying Carol Dweck's work on mindsets. She says we all have one of two mindsets in every area of our lives, and in every experience. She also says that our mindset is fluid and can change. I realized through studying her work that I had a fixed mindset most of my life. Meaning I viewed everything as a performance, a test, and you either passed or failed. In this mindset it was all about looking good and passing the test.

What I was trying to adopt was a growth mindset, which believes that everything that happens to me is in my best interest and an opportunity to learn and grow. Believe me. In that moment sitting in the hospital bed it was incredibly hard to make myself have a growth mindset, but it was also a watershed moment in my life.

And here is the thing: **LIFE PUNCHES EVERYONE IN THE FACE!!**

I sincerely hope it isn't a guy who is 6'4 240lbs, but it is an absolute guarantee that life is going to punch you in the face. The job economy is the worst it has been in decades. Most college graduates can't get a job and are moving back in with their parents. Bad things happen in relationships. Over fifty percent of marriages are ending in divorce, and that's with fewer and fewer couples even making it to the alter. Infidelity is rampant in our culture. We are losing loved ones to cancer and other diseases. Life is going to punch us in the face, and we get to decide whether we are going to have a victim mindset or a growth mindset. We can be lieve there is nothing we can do and that we are just a victim of circumstance and just stay tied to that tree.

"I got fired again."
"No one will support my dream."
"I haven't sold one thing all month."
"No one will pay me what I'm worth."
"I'm not deserving of a healthy relationship."
"It doesn't matter what I do, it never works out."
"My coach won't play me."

OR

We can adopt a growth mindset and believe no matter what happens to me, it is in my best interest and an opportunity to learn and grow. We can ask, "What is one thing I can do to make this better?" Which mindset are you going to adopt?

I will make you this promise: If you will adopt a growth mindset in every area of your life, you will become an unstoppable force. How do you stop someone who has that growth mindset? How do you stop someone who can get knocked out by a guy who is 6'4" 240lbs, BUT who believes that is in their best interest and an opportunity to learn and grow?!

YOU CAN'T!

What is the alternative? To believe it is in your worst interest? All that does is put you in a victim mentality and all but guarantee that you will experience more of those things in the future.

Obviously, I don't want you or I to get punched in the face, and if I could go backwards I would do things differently. BUT we can't go backwards in life! We can only move forward. So, the most beneficial thing we can do is adopt a growth mindset and believe everything that happens to us is in our best interest and an opportunity to learn and grow. We can't control what has happened, but we do have 100% control over the meaning we give the events in our lives. *You might achieve some "success," but you will never reach your full potential without sacrifice, perseverance, hustle, AND a growth mindset.*

A couple weeks after I got knocked out and I still had two black eyes, I hesitantly shared with one of my clients on our weekly call what had happened. Much to my surprise, he was actually told me he was glad that happened to me. (Thanks man!) He told me that I always made things sound so easy, and he was grateful to know that I am human just like him and that I struggle to.

It has turned out over the years that sharing that story is one of the most impactful things in people's lives at speaking engagements. My authentic vulnerability ironically makes people trust me more, and helps me have a greater impact on their life. But I had to stop trying to hide my weaknesses and shortcomings, and bring them into the light and focus on learning, growing, and getting better from them.

It's not easy, but adopting a growth mindset is one of the most beneficial things you can ever do. *(P.S. You must have a growth mindset about having a growth mindset. It is going to take time and a lot of effort to adopt a growth mindset as your normal mode of operation.)*

When you really start to hustle you are going to get knocked out a lot by life. You'll have friends that try and sabotage you. You'll experience many situations where it feels like everyone and everything in life are against you. In those moments it will be very easy to have a fixed mindset and believe you failed the test, or to try and hide all your shortcomings and failures. My challenge to you is to keep pushing, because when it feels like everything in life is conspiring against you that usually means you are on the midst of a massive break through.

Never give up.
Never give in.
No matter how many times you get knocked down, get back up and give it everything you have once again.

Watch Eric Thomas video "TGIM The Truth Behind MSU's win over Michigan."

CHAPTER 28

The Quickest Path To Becoming Ignored

One of my friends got a text the other day from an old buddy asking if he could take my friend out to lunch. My friend hadn't heard from this guy since his wedding a few years back. Great, right?

Except his "friend" sells insurance and investment products now.

My friend said he had a pretty good idea of how the lunch would go since the guy's dad (who also sells insurance) had already tried the same thing a couple years back.

I may not know a lot, but I do know one thing for sure, unequivocally, and without a single doubt: *the quickest way to become ignored in the world is to continually ask people to give you stuff.*

This hit me the other day when I was walking down the Third Street Promenade in Santa Monica. In Los Angeles we have a lot of people who live on the street. I hate using this as an example, because I believe that poverty is a multifaceted beast and not a simple cause and effect issue. Eugene Cho says that one of the biggest challenges of living on the street is that people start to ignore you, and eventually you come to think you don't exist or matter. I'm pretty sure that is not a conducive mindset to ever getting off the street.

But here is what hit me: one of the main reasons people living on the street get ignored is because they're always asking for something. The predominant question being asked is, "What will you give me?"

Unfortunately, that is also the fastest possible path to becoming ignored.

If you're reading this, then chances are you probably aren't asking people for change on the street. However, in my experience many people have a strangely similar mindset.

I can't tell you how many people I come across whose predominant question is, "What will the world give me today?"

Are there any good jobs left out there?
Is my boss in another bad mood today?
Will anyone actually buy our products?
Will the cost of living continue to get higher?
Will I win the lottery today?

This type of mindset will eventually leave you ignored and left behind in our world.

What if we focused instead on how we could provide more value or a useful service to people around us? *What if our dominant question became, "What can I give, create, or share with the world today?"*

How can I add value to this person's life? How can I add value to this group?

I'm not saying you should avoid charging, making money, being well compensated, or anything else, but I am suggesting that you provide so much value that people actually want to compensate you well! Instead of trying to sell your product or yourself, what if you tried to give something valuable away? What is something that you could create, or already have available, that you could actively *give* to people who need it?

Given the amount of influence and opportunity we have, people are often shocked that *Train to be CLUTCH* is as young as it is, and is only run by

Jamie and myself. But one of the main reasons we have such influence and so many opportunities is without a doubt tied to our constant focus on meeting real needs, providing tons of value to people's lives, and treating them like people and not production units.

No matter what business you are in, or want to be in, you can do the same.

No one was more underqualified then I was when I started out. No money. No psychology degree. No experience.

I just did the best I could with what I had, right where I was.

You can:

Write an article about what you wish you would have known starting out.
Make an app.
Find people to mentor.
Experiment with solutions to problems inside your company (without being asked).
Share ideas with people you want to work with.
Write a short book and sell it on *iBooks and Kindle.*
Shoot a video on your phone.
Write a marketing plan for your dream company, and just give it away to them.
Write down ten ideas for your dream company to work for and send it to them.

Honestly, it doesn't really matter what it is that you do. What matters greatly is that you focus on giving, experimenting, and solving real world problems. Everything in your life will start to turn around. Not overnight, but over time, *if* your heart posture shifts to what you can give instead of what you can get.

"You can have whatever you want in life if you will help enough people get what they want." — Zig Ziglar

CHAPTER 29

"Those Destined For Greatness, Must First Walk Alone In The Desert"
- Winston Churchill

We live in a culture that is absolutely obsessed with achievement. Thanks to the bright lights of television, many of us are so enamored with the idea of "making it" that we forget what it takes to actually get there. In the era of steroids, cheating scandals, Enron, and "instant" everything, we've lost an appreciation for the desert. According to studies done by Harvard, the greatest predictor of future success is the ability to delay gratification. Put another way, the greatest predictor of future success is the ability to hustle in the desert.

The desert is where you're forced to battle the negativity in your head that tells you you will never make it, you are a fraud, and everyone is going to find out.

The desert is where it seems everyone is telling you to give up your dreams. The desert is where your failures are all anyone wants to talk about. The desert is where it seems you are crazy for pursuing the dream planted deep inside your heart.

The desert is where you learn to fall in love with the journey, not the results. The desert is where you learn that failure is a learning tool, and an inescapable part of becoming who you are destined to be. The desert is where you learn that the greatest lessons come from failure, not success. The desert is where you learn to fall in love with the *process* of becoming great.

The desert is where a lot of people turn their backs on you. The desert is where your true character is not only tested, but refined.

The desert is where we learn to put first things first. The desert is where we learn people are so much more important than achievement. The desert is where we learn to trust in God rather than people.

The desert is a graveyard of dreams buried by people who weren't willing to develop their hustle muscle.

No one can escape the desert. Some might spend more time there than others, but much like *the path to mastery*, the desert applies to everyone. It is unavoidable.

Even Jesus didn't avoid the desert. Before He stepped into His public ministry, He went to the desert and was tempted by the Devil while fasting for forty days.

Derrick Coleman won a Super Bowl with the Seahawks, but not after going un-drafted and facing a complete lack of belief by anyone else that a deaf man could play in the NFL. In many ways, he is always in his desert.

Michael Jordan went through his desert after being cut from his high school team.

Peyton Manning went through his desert as he was overcoming 2 neck surgeries and having to totally re-learn how to throw a football.

Steve Jobs went through his desert for more than a decade after being fired from Apple, until they finally begged him to come back and save the company he created.

Walt Disney went through his desert after being fired from a local Kansas City newspaper for "lacking creativity."

The Beatles went through their desert while playing set after set in German strip clubs for boisterous patrons.

I went through my desert after Duke, when I moved to LA and lived in a homeless shelter for six months, then the closet of a gym for nine months, and then cut out almost everything in my life for another six to nine months to study and read like a med student.

Some think that you become great on the big stage under the bright lights, but the bright lights only reveal your hustle in the desert. Churchill was right: "Those destined for greatness must first walk alone in the desert." Embrace your desert, instead of running from it. There is no better place to develop your hustle than in the desert. Most will avoid it at all costs, but the few who embrace it will step into their greatness and change the world.

CHAPTER 30

Make. Believe.

"Make. Believe." I have always been fascinated by this slogan from Sony. Ever since I became aware of it I've loved it, even though I'm still not sure if I completely grasp it.

If you look around wherever you're sitting, I bet you'll see a lot of things that didn't exist one hundred, fifty, twenty-five, maybe even as few as five years ago.

Someone had to imagine it, and then create it.

Do you know how many times I have sat with someone who is world-class at their craft and made up some exercise for them to experiment with? Honestly, it's too many to count.

I don't do this recklessly, and I don't usually tell them, "No one has ever tried this before," and there is always some piece of research I've studied that makes me think it could work. But in the moment, I just make it up. Then I go back to them a few weeks or months later and check in on their progress.

If it works, great! I share it with others and observe the effects. If it doesn't work, great! We tweak it or throw it out and start another experiment.

When I created the first mental training apps in the world for basketball, soccer and golf, I had no clue what I was doing. Truthfully, I thought they sucked, but a lot of people loved them. I even had people who didn't play the sports they were designed for use them and tell me they helped them in something completely unrelated!

I make stuff up. I often think it sucks. Inevitably, some people think it's awesome.

I'm not responsible for how it is received. I am only responsible for doing the work.

Don't get caught up in the uncontrollables.
Make. Believe.
Do. The. *Work.*
Chop wood. Carry Water.
Hustle.

CHAPTER 31

Become A Resource Hub

What would it look like if you became one of the go-to resource hubs for your industry?

Too many times I think people focus on selling and recruiting instead of serving and equipping.

One of the reasons I think *Train to be CLUTCH* has blown up is because we are constantly trying to find more ways to serve and provide value to our existing base, rather than just expanding to more people. Technology has made this so much easier than ever before, and it can be as simple as taking fifteen minutes to write out the ten most important lessons you've learned.

We did this with someone we mentor, a person who plays professional soccer. Interestingly, even though she rarely played for her team, after she tweeted the lessons, it got picked up and published by two different magazines.

Every single one of us has valuable wisdom to share, but too often we think we don't have much to offer or we think we're too busy to do things like that. The crazy part to me is that if you spent more time providing value and creating a resource hub for others, you would almost never have to sell or recruit. People would be lining up at your door.

So, where can you start?

Offer to mentor someone who wants to do what you do.

Write an article about the most important lessons you learned in the last year.

Share your highlights from a great book.

Just get in the habit of sharing wisdom with those who are seeking it. Always remember though, "The difference between a pest and a guest is an invitation." Starting with your circle of friends is probably not a good place. Find people who *want* to do what you do, and are open to hearing what you're saying.

Don't wait, either. You will always feel a little bit uncomfortable, no matter your age or level of expertise. I know a guy who serves in one of the highest positions in the NBA, a man tens of thousands of people look to for wisdom, and he *still* doesn't think he's ready to write a book.

Extract and share the wisdom in the moment. It's more powerful that way.

Jamie and I have *never* focused on selling. But we've *always* focused on *serving and providing value.* As a byproduct, we've built a million-dollar brand. We've become a resource hub that attracts people from all over the world, and you can too, but it will take a shift in heart posture from what can you get, to what can you *give.*

"When you put first things first, second things are not suppressed, they increase." -C.S. Lewis

CHAPTER 32

The American Dream, A Trailer Park And A Vanderbilt Sociology Class

When I got to Vanderbilt I was nowhere close to prepared for the academic environment. On my residence hall alone, three people had gotten perfect scores on the ACT.

I never took the SAT, but I got a 21 on the ACT, and because I was an athlete I was able to combine my scores, which got me up to a whopping 22 out of 36. To put this into perspective, with a 22 I would've had a hard time getting into one of the state schools in Oklahoma.

So, I got in as a "slot student." One of the twenty or so kids the athletic department can get in every year that are not qualified academically, but who have the potential to be a game changer athletically for their sports program.

One day I was sitting in my sociology class and my teacher said something that really frustrated me. Basically, she said that the "American Dream" was dead, and that social mobility was extinct in our society.

After the class I approached her and told her that she was flat out wrong. I shared how my dad grew up in a trailer park, yet became one of the most successful eye surgeons in Oklahoma.

She told me that that was an anecdotal story, and did not fairly represent social mobility for our society as a whole.

Maybe she was right.
Maybe the American Dream is dead.
Maybe social mobility is like winning the lottery.
You hear about people winning the lottery, but the majority of people lose.

My argument is that the American Dream is far from dead, but it might as well be, because the American hustle, grit, and willingness to sacrifice that used to embody our society has seemingly become as rare as the sight of an endangered white tiger.

CHAPTER 33

Anyone Left Who Will Hustle?!

At the beginning of Kevin Hart's *Laugh At My Pain* DVD, right before he goes onstage, he does a chant with his team.

Kevin says, "Everyone wanna be famous."

Then his crew says, "Nobody wanna put the work in."

They repeat this four or five times. Everyone wants to be famous, but nobody wants to put the work in.

A recent poll revealed that a majority of kids would rather be the assistant to a famous person than a doctor, lawyer, or astronaut. I'll leave to others the social commentary about what that means for our country, and I will just address what I experience.

I have friends who tell me, "Man! I would love to have your job." Or, "I would love to do what you do." My response is always the same, "No you don't. You want the perks, not the responsibility!" They don't want to sacrifice, hustle and grind like I have (and continue to do). They wouldn't live and serve in a homeless shelter, and they definitely wouldn't live in the closet of a gym.

I always tell them that the homeless shelter is still taking interns. As far as I know, not a single person has ever taken me up. It sounds cool on paper, but most people would rather get coffee for a person who has put in all the dirty, hard work than actually get their own hands dirty. You love movies where the hero goes through adversity and comes out stronger, but you don't want to experience adversity on your own. You love the stories of people who get told "no" over and over again and keep on persisting, but you give up after the second or third "no."

The real key to unlocking your personal greatness is a willingness to say "Yes" to what most people say "No way" to, and a willingness to say, "No," to what most people say "Yes" to.

Be willing to do what most people won't for long enough, and eventually you will be living like most people can't.

CHAPTER 34

"People Are Fake"

That was my hard and fast belief during my college days, along with its inherent partner, "but I am real." However, after some serious introspection and self-awareness, I realized I was actually a *real* jerk who created a lot of *real* pain in people's lives.

When I first moved to Los Angeles, my best friend drove me crazy. He didn't seem to really care about people at all behind the scenes, but he treated people like kings and queens to their faces. Everyone loved him, and most people thought I was a jerk!

I would think, "How ridiculous is this? I'm the one who *actually* cares about people and they think I'm a jerk. He doesn't, but they think he walks on water." Then, one day it hit me: if you *actually* care about people, and you have seen and heard people tell him that seeing him is the highlight of their week, shouldn't you *act* like you care about people? This was incredibly challenging for me, because I thought it was being *fake*.

This truth solidified for me one day when I was running one of my first *Train to be CLUTCH* workshops. One of the guys in the workshop ran a store and he felt the same way I did about "faking" it. He preferred to keep it real with people.

I asked him, "Who do you get really excited about when they come into your store? I mean, when this person comes in, you know it's going to be a great day, and they make you feel amazing."

He thought about it for a couple minutes, and then he said, "I never thought about it like that. The guy who I always want to see comes in with a huge smile, warm energy, treats me super well, and he does this no matter what is going on in his life."

I asked if he was that guy in other people's lives. He shook his head and said, "Sadly, I think I'm the opposite."

What do people consistently get when they encounter you? Do they get love, joy, hope, peace, and patience? Do they get anger, frustration, manipulation, "it's never good enough," complaining, bitterness, and jealousy?

The good news for us is that we can deliberately train ourselves to treat people in a positive way. Will it feel uncomfortable and like we are faking it in the beginning? *Without a shadow of a doubt!*

But do you think LeBron and Kobe are thrilled to wake up and go pound on their body for 5 or 6 hours every day? No way! They are deliberately training and disciplining their bodies to be able to perform on command. We can do the exact same thing with developing true mental toughness and other characteristics we weren't "born" with.

Is it hard? Absolutely!
Do I still fail at it all the time? Absolutely!
Is it worth it? Absolutely!

And above all, it's not fake. It's *deliberate* and *intentional* discipline and training to treat people the way we want to be treated and to develop the characteristics we want to embody.

CHAPTER 35

Work Smarter, Not Harder

A few years ago, there was a guy who was starting out in the mental conditioning space just like I was, and he was doing a lot of work.

How do I know this?

It felt like every day he was putting out a new track or video that he had created. He was creating all sorts of content, and I saw this because I followed him on Twitter. On multiple occasions I reached out to him, and let him know that I could help him. I showed him that even though he was creating all sorts of content, it wasn't getting anywhere: his social media Klout score was a 45 and mine was a 67. At the end of the day, he wasn't willing to listen, and he continued to flounder because of it.

Hopefully, he has started to figure it out by now, but honestly, I don't think he has.

You see, some people think it is all about working harder, that the key to success is "just work harder." That is flat out wrong and, in fact, that can end up killing you.

Just ask Urban Meyer. His dad had taught him that the key to success was to just outwork everyone, and that any problem could be solved with more effort. When Urban woke up in a hospital after collapsing from stress, his doctors told him that if he didn't drastically change his lifestyle, he would kill himself. More effort wasn't the key to his success; it was actually the thing that could have taken him away from those he loved most. I'm all for working hard, hustling, and taking full advantage of your 86,400 seconds every day, but you also need to make sure you're using excellent strategies as well.

Did you know that Warren Buffett starts his days with six hours of reading? Reading is one of the quickest ways to learn from the greats who have gone before us, which is a fantastic idea since history tends to repeat itself. Warren Buffett's track record in the investment world is virtually unparalleled. Last time I checked, his financial net worth was fourth in the world.

I can already hear the excuses flying around your head now. *Just stop, please.*

I can't tell you how many people say, "I don't have time to read." The sad thing to me is that you can't afford *not* to read. If anyone has ample opportunity to justify *not* spending quality time reading every day, it is the guy who literally has billions of dollars on the line every single day, but ironically I believe that's one of the main reasons Mr. Buffett *does* spend so much time reading.

I wonder what would happen if all the (good) reasons we make for not having enough time, became our justification for why we MUST make ample time to read.

Because I have 3 kids, I must seek wisdom.
Because I am the CEO of this company, I must seek wisdom.
Because I am responsible for managing 35 people, I must seek wisdom.

People often think I'm brilliant because of how much I read and study. Trust me, I'm not brilliant. In fact, a case could probably be made that I'm not even that smart (remember that ACT score of 22?). But because of how much I read, I've developed intellectual capacities, thoughts, and ideas that I never would've developed had I not made a serious commitment to reading.

Reading is your secret weapon to change both who you become, and the overall trajectory of your life. The best part is that since so few people read, it's actually pretty easy to get ahead when you do.

Hustle in ways others won't so that eventually you can do what others can't.

P.S.: Not all books are created equal. (The people who take on our reading challenge never come out the same.) t2bc.com/challenge

In our first book, Burn Your Goals, we wrote about *The Path to Mastery,* as well as the *Road Signs on The Path to Mastery,* but one of the keys to the path to mastery is making sure that you're getting <u>expert</u> coaching.

Research on expert performance confirms the relationship between elite performance and coaching. In his New York Times bestseller *One Thing,* Gary Keller observes that, "The single most important difference between... amateurs and... elite performers is that the future elite per-formers seek out teachers and coaches and engage in supervised training, whereas the amateurs rarely engage in similar types of practice. Find a coach. You'll be hard-pressed to find anyone who achieves extraordinary results without one"

This is why so many people experience tremendous transformation, growth, and results in their life after going through our 1-on-1 mentorship program. If you can't afford a program like that, you can always create a mastermind group of like-minded people and study the wisdom of great mentors by reading and discussing their books, videos, and other tools they put out.

Today, there are a lot of people who claim to be social media experts, but when I look at their personal social media presence, they have very little influence. Why would I want to take advice from someone who's lost? Maybe I'm crazy, but that just seems dumb. I want to learn from someone who doesn't just have head knowledge, but is actually building some-thing with the "wisdom" they're dispensing.

In a world where most of the gatekeepers no longer wield the power they once did, too often coaching and mentorship can devolve into the blind leading the blind, whether that's in business, finance, sports, teaching, or other areas. Make sure that the people you're learning from are expert *practitioners* of what they're suggesting you do. I don't know about you, but I'm not taking health and fitness advice from someone who is obese. Nor will I ever take business advice from someone who's never run a successful business.

You can accelerate your growth and avoid a lot of undue pain and frustration if you seek out the wisdom of experts who have gone before you.

My advice to the guy at the beginning of this chapter would have been to stop focusing on creating new content, and instead to start stewarding what he had already created. I created the greatest mental training presence in the world on Twitter with basically only one short video. My strategy was to get it into as many people's hands as possible, by targeting them with @ mentions that included the video. No one did this, and quite frankly, very few people use this strategy to provide value today.

It worked incredibly well, and it's most likely why you're reading this book and have been influenced by me. It all started with that strategy, and most of our opportunities today link back in one way or another to my initial Twitter strategy.

Like many of the best strategies, it was a simple one. But simple rarely means easy. Even if something is easy to do, that also means it is easy *not* to do.

Additionally, I seek out people who aren't just great at what they do, but who are also the type of person I want to *become*. Because at the end of the day, I don't want to just be a great businessman or mentor; I want to be a great husband, father, and friend. And so, those are qualities I seek out as well.

Don't just work harder, work smarter, and that starts with hustling to gain wisdom with a passionate fervor that would make Socrates smile :)

CHAPTER 36

Greatness Is Made In The Oven, Not The Microwave

There is no such thing as microwavable greatness. But thanks to societal conditioning and the simple realities of human nature, we've been conditioned to believe there is, instead of relying on an appreciation for the process. No longer do we enjoy the journey, we just want to pop it in the microwave and watch greatness come out two minutes later.

But that isn't how greatness works. Greatness is more like an oven than a microwave.

It seems to me that nowadays people only do something to get something. The "experts" say, "Start with your end goal in mind, and then work backwards." Sadly, the end goal is usually some outcome that's practically meaningless in the grand scheme of life, instead of something real and lasting, like the type of person you become.

Francis Chan said, "Our greatest fear in life should not be failure. Our greatest fear should be succeeding at things in life that don't really matter."

Sometimes I wonder if life is designed to bring about a real heart posture shift from what we can get to what we can give. If we're starting with the end in mind, then all we are trying to do is manipulate the system to give us what we want. But what if we have no clue what we truly want, or more importantly, what's best for us?

I don't know about you, but some of the most incredible things in life were things I never could have articulated. On the flip side, many of the things I got that I wanted so badly, ended up fading away and seeming so worthless after the fact.

I think that life is a journey of trust, and if we trust God and remain faithful, He will take us on an incredible journey we could never have dreamed of. One thing I am sure of is that God's plan for my life is a better plan than anything I can come up with. It rarely feels like that in the moment, but if I stop and really think about His track record, I quickly realize that His plan and track record are MUCH better than mine.

When I first began building Train to be CLUTCH on Twitter, I often heard business people ask, "Yes, but what is the ROI (Return On Investment) of social media?"

Social media didn't fit into their neat boxes for marketing.

Gary Vaynerchuk put it this way, asking, "What is the ROI of your mother?" You can't put a number on it. It is immeasurable.

What I found is that it's not linear, and it's not quick, but it is immeasurably powerful.

Here is a non-linear example of the power of Twitter:

Our strategy has always been to send people @ mentions with valuable tools in them. I sent Alan Stein multiple tweets with a video, and he didn't respond at first. Then one day, Alan responded very positively to a tweet with a video I sent him. Shortly thereafter, he endorsed our mental training app for basketball.

About nine months later, Jon Gordon reached out to Alan and asked him who was the best in the world in mental training. Alan told him that I was. Jon reached out to me and asked me to work with his son on mental training.

A few months later I was on Twitter using my normal Twitter strategy and I had sent an @ mention with a video to the @coaching_u Twitter account. Since Jon Gordon followed both me and @coaching_u, the tweet showed up on his timeline. He then sent me a text message with the contact info for the guys who run *Coaching U*. After talking with them, they asked if I was interested in being a guest on their podcast. I ended up doing the podcast with them a few months later, and the podcast episodes went like this:

Jay Bilas
Billy Donavan
Joshua Medcalf
Shaka Smart

It wasn't linear, but all of a sudden my name was beside some of the biggest names in basketball. Over fifty thousand people listen to their podcast, and that episode established me in the basketball world as one of the top experts in mental training.

Success is rarely linear, and real success is never going to happen overnight. Enjoy all the twists and turns in your journey, and you will be on your way to falling in love with the process of becoming great!

It takes around six months to build a Rolls Royce and only thirteen hours to build a Toyota. Patience is a struggle for me, but I also know what I'm building.

CHAPTER 37

Leveraging Twitter

When I did my workshop with UNC Women's Soccer, I'm not ashamed to say that I absolutely crushed it. The girls loved it, and they were really excited. A few of them even told me that the national team needed to hear me!

One of them told me she was starving before my two and a half hour presentation, but afterwards she told me that as soon as I started speaking, she completely forgot about how hungry she was! So, imagine my surprise after this workshop when only four of the girls started following me on Twitter! But I thought I knew why.

I came home from that trip and I told the guy who helped me with web and business stuff that I had to figure out Twitter, and it had to happen now. A few of my friends at the time had experimented with paying different companies to help them get more followers, but nothing was guaranteed. One company we found even wanted $4,500 a month. At this point, I was only making $1,500 during my best months!

Eventually my friend told me about a company he found that guaranteed 10,000 followers for $118. I was immediately sold! I paid the money, and four days later the followers started rolling in by the hundreds. Overnight, three of my friends who all had somewhat high-profile Twitter presences began following me.

What changed? The *perception* did.

Imagine the confusion when you experience a workshop, performance, or product that you think is amazing, and then you find out that only 255 people follow them on Twitter. In my opinion, that was exactly what happened with the girls at UNC. After seeing that I had so few followers on Twitter, I think there's a high probability that they questioned their experience and my credibility, *even though they had loved it.*

Eventually, I realized that what I bought were 'fake robot' accounts, but it didn't matter. People didn't know that, and they were now much more interested in the quality of the content that I was sending them, because in their mind I had to be legit if I had tens of thousands of followers. As I sent out videos and provided value to people, a lot of them started to follow me, so I started to gain a lot of authentic followers, and fast.

I also was able to build up social currency by retweeting and mentioning other people in my tweets. One day I got an email that a guy had retweeted my video to his 90k plus followers, and I was over the moon! Immediately, I realized I had that same power, and I could make other people feel similarly by retweeting their tweets.

Ten to fifteen years ago, and probably still today, people would pay a lot of money for a mailing list that had contact information for a certain demographic. For example, if I was interested in targeting people in the Los Angeles soccer world, I could reach out to *Eurosport* and try and buy their list of people who get their soccer magazine every month who also live in Los Angeles.

On Twitter you can get access to very similar lists. All I did, was track down the high-volume Twitter accounts of people and brands who would seemingly be interested in mental conditioning, leadership, and life skills training. Then, I simply went down their list of followers and sent each of them a copy and paste message with my speaking reel.

The tweet would say, "This 7min video on mental training could help take your game to the next level (Video link) #traintobeclutch" It was a very simple and straightforward strategy. Target people in my target demographic with a valuable video that could greatly benefit their lives.

Many people used very colorful language to let me know they didn't ap preciate my strategy, but a lot more people told me that the video had really opened their eyes and impacted their life. If your Klout score is above 50, it puts you in the top 5% of all people on Twitter. Well, within six months I went from having zero presence on Twitter to a Klout score over 70. In half a year, I had built the greatest mental training presence in the world on Twitter.

Around four months in to using this strategy, I got a direct message from Cori Close, who is the head coach of UCLA Women's Basketball. She asked if she could take me to lunch. During lunch, she asked if I was interested in heading up the mental conditioning elements of her pro- gram. That was over three years ago, and the majority of our influence and opportunities are all linked back to Twitter in one way or another. The crazy thing to me is that even though I have shared this strategy with countless people, I almost never see people use it!

Some people consider it spam, but I don't believe it is spam if it is truly something that could benefit other people's lives. I wish more people did this for me. Imagine if every day four or five people sent you some really valuable video, article, mp3, or book highlights. The thing about this strategy is even though it is simple, it requires dirty, hard work, and most people simply aren't willing to do that. Hopefully, you aren't one of those people.

You don't even have to be the expert. You can share great content from other people, and eventually you're going to have a ton of influence as a person who is a trusted source for great content! That's all Google does. You and I go to them and they tell us where to go.

What is stopping you from becoming that? I've already done it. Now it's *your* turn.

"Often the best way to make friends and customers for life is to direct them to a better service or product than yours. Be the source of valuable information rather than the source of your 'product of the day.'" — James Altucher

CHAPTER 38

Believing The Lie

I hated my voice growing up.

I'm not sure exactly when it hit me, but probably about seventh grade. I realized at that moment that singing soprano was *not* a good thing for a guy. It was as if someone switched on a light, and all of sudden society's judgments and stereotypes about masculinity were staring me in the face.

My voice never really cracked when I went through puberty, it just slowly lowered a few octaves. However, I never developed a deep voice, and I was terribly insecure about it. In church, my friends told me they hated sitting next to me, because my voice was terrible when I would sing. In high school, my close friends relentlessly teased me about my "cool stories." *Eventually, it got to the point where I decided it was safer not to open my mouth.* At least that way I wouldn't get made fun of.

I heard Judah Smith say that his dad told him every day that people wanted to hear what he had to say. For a very long time, I believed the exact opposite about myself. The worst was when I would hear my voice played back on a tape or video recording. It was painful to hear, and painful to watch.

I'll never forget the day I walked into Robin Pingeton's office at Missouri to do a workshop with her team. After we exchanged formal introductions she said, "It's amazing! Your voice sounds exactly like it does on your *iTunes* spoken word album! You have the most incredible voice!"

I had believed the lies for so long it was hard to believe the truth. Not only did people love to hear me tell stories, *they loved to hear my voice.*

To this day, fear still gets in the way of opening my mouth sometimes. Not surprisingly though, I tell my best stories when I open my mouth. I don't tell my best stories when I sit down at a computer to write. I tell my best stories when I choose to operate out of love and not out of fear, and I open my mouth and speak. It's still not easy for me, but I have learned that if I want to fulfill my destiny I am going to have to consistently act in spite of my fear, and open my mouth. The more I operate out of love, the easier it gets.

I think the evil one has a vested interest in making you believe your greatest asset is your greatest weakness. Don't believe the lie.

CHAPTER 39

Dirty, Hard Work

"Everyone thinks that greatness is sexy, it's not. It is dirty hard work." —
Ben Hogan

Calling all one hundred and eighty collegiate women's golf coaches attending an event we were speaking at was not easy, especially when we only had five days before the event. It was a simple strategy, but it was dirty hard work.

A lot of people are looking for a complex strategy, a new system, or some other fancy plan to help them succeed. The reality is that it's a commitment to doing the dirty hard work that is going to get you where you want to go. It's not complex or fancy. It is a commitment to doing the dirty work that is going to help you mold and shape your character into the person you want to become. It's simple stuff, but simple isn't easy.

It wasn't a complex marketing strategy to call all those coaches before the WGCA event in Las Vegas. It was countercultural to not try and sell them anything. All we did was ask them, "What is you mission in coaching? What is your mission for your program? We are here to serve you, so let us know if there is anything we can do to help you, regardless of whether you can ever hire us out to work with your program. We create lots of free tools for coaches and players every week, and we just want to equip you in any way we can."

We were told no one had ever called all the coaches before and not tried to sell them anything. The people who called were always trying to sell them something. One of the coaches even apologized for not calling us back, "I'm so sorry for not calling you back, I thought my players were playing a practical joke on me. I didn't think there was any way you guys were actually calling every coach here." Never had two of the event's main speakers taken the time to call each coach. Why? Because that's a whole lot of dirty hard work. We got up three hours earlier than normal and stayed up later every night in order to call every coach, while still handling our day-to-day responsibilities. We also called all the assistant coaches, because we didn't want them to feel left out.

Was it incredibly hard? Yes.

Did we want to give up at times? Yes.

Were some of the coaches rude to us? Yes.

Did Jamie lose his voice? Yes.

But was it worth it? Most definitely!

We built some incredible relationships, and as a byproduct of doing the dirty hard work and actually caring about the people, we have the second or third most influential consulting brand in women's golf. We put first things first, and second things were not suppressed. Second things increased!

TRAIN To Be Clutch

- What are some actions that are 100% under your control that you could be faithful in doing?
- What are most other people on your team or in your field not willing to do?
- How much growth could you experience by having a willingness to do the dirty hard work?

CHAPTER 40

Freedom

I had a very warped view of God growing up. For most of my childhood my parents and I were heavily involved in the Southern Baptist church, and on top of that I received what felt like very conditional love from my father. I quickly came to believe that God was disappointed with me the majority of the time.

Then, when I was sixteen, something happened. A mentor came into my life and started sharing with us that believe it or not, Jesus wasn't concerned with us cussing or drinking alcohol. Jesus wanted a relationship with us, not a bunch of rules. It was about our hearts, not religion or behavior. My friends and I couldn't believe this. It blew our minds, and what he shared with us eventually got him blacklisted from our church, where some folks literally called him the "anti-Christ."

I'm so grateful he had the courage to share with us what I've come to believe is the truth about Jesus and God. He started me on the journey to having a real relationship with Jesus.

The next monumental moment of freedom came the first time I heard Judah Smith preach in Los Angeles. My friend Ryan invited me to come to "Bible Study" one day when we were playing golf, and my life has never been the same. Judah started unpacking things about the Bible, God, and Jesus I had never heard taught anywhere, ever. He shared every week how the Bible is basically a huge love story of God's radical, reckless, and unconditional love for you and me (not exactly what I was taught growing up in the rules-based Southern Baptist churches).

One of my favorite stories (my modern day paraphrase) that explains the whole story of the Bible is about this dude who was a pastor back in the day, and one day God tells him to marry a woman who makes a living having sex with men.

The pastor is like, "Whoa God! I don't think that is a good look for a pastor! Do you know what they'll write about me on Twitter? Do you understand the pictures they will post on the 'gram? The memes about me will blow up the internet! I think you got this one all wrong, God!"

The pastor eventually relents and marries the prostitute. They end up having a few kids, life is as good as it can be, and then the woman leaves the pastor to return to her old life of prostitution.

After a while, God tells the pastor to go get his wife out of prostitution and bring her back home. You can only imagine the pastor's response at this point!

"For real, God?! Do you know how much I suffered to begin with? Do you understand the emotional pain I've been through because of this woman who abandoned me and our three kids?"

Once again, the pastor eventually relents and goes to find his wife.

He finds her, but when he tries to rescue her, he is told that he must purchase her. The men don't care who he thinks she is. She belongs to them, and if he wants her, he'll have to pay for her freedom.

He pays the men, and takes her home once again.

In case that story was hard to follow, you and I are the woman, and Jesus is the pastor. The Bible is full of story after story after story like this, describing how much God loves us. Every time Jesus encountered the broken, downtrodden, and outcast members of society, He healed them, and showered them with reckless love and grace. Jesus said that if you have seen Him, then you have seen the Father.

When I started to understand that there was nothing I could do to make God love me any more, and nothing I could do to make Him love me any less, I started to experience true freedom.

All I need to do is trust Him and His finished work. He already paid the price for my life and my sin, and once I realize I have nothing to prove and only freedom to live, love, and create, it is such an incredible experience that frees not just my soul itself, but my identity and my potential to do my best work.

Living every day wondering whether or not the person who created the world is mad at you is a weight no person is meant to carry. I truly believe understanding and experiencing the relentless love of Jesus is the greatest power in the entire world. I also believe that trying to operate outside that freedom makes it truly impossible to become the greatest version of yourself.

The most powerful force in the universe loves you, so you are free to conquer the world. Perfect love casts out fear, and His love for you is perfect. He wants you to experience the perpetual rest that comes from understanding His finished work on the cross and never to worry about anything because of knowing who holds your future.

CHAPTER 41

Stop "Networking"

This past summer, I was speaking to a group of "young leaders" in an organization, and this is what I told them…

I can't tell you why our brand has blown up. I can't tell you why people who are the best in the world at their craft, listen to us. What I can tell you is what we did, and sometimes more importantly, what we didn't do.

And it definitely didn't happen because we "networked."

When I hear the word, it makes me want to vomit. Maybe it's because I've lived in L.A. for my entire professional life, and L.A. is a place where the majority of people seem to be trying to constantly use anyone and everyone to further their own personal interests. Something about that has made "networking" a dirty word to me.

I would suggest that rather than networking, you start *investing* in people. It doesn't really matter how many people you "know." It matters how many people hold you in very high regard. I "know" a lot of people, but I would recommend very few of them. My approach has always been simply to ask people what their dream is, and how I can help. When I first started out, I didn't have a lot to offer, but I found it to be true that if this becomes your dominant mode of operation, over time you'll be able to offer a lot more. Most professional communities are very small, and one of the greatest keys to success is becoming known as the type of person who is constantly investing in others. I don't ever have to worry about getting opportunities, because of how much value I constantly provide the world around me.

Your whole life would change if you would simply start to focus on becoming a trusted resource for others. It's amazing how my phone blows up when people get fired. It's much better to focus on becoming that resource hub while you have a job. That way, if you get fired, there will be people lining up to fight over hiring you.

We're talking simple stuff, too. If you made a commitment to send out every great article or book you came across to twenty-five people in your industry who are around the country, your opportunities would grow exponentially, I promise.

Most people are so selfishly focused on survival that they never pull their heads out of the sand and realize there is a world of opportunity around them if they would just focus on serving and adding value to others.

This quote is worth repeating…

"You can have everything in life you want if you will just help enough people get what they want." — Zig Ziglar

CHAPTER 42

What Would You Do If You Were The Leader Of A World Changing Organization?

What would you do if you were the...

Best coach in the world?
Best spouse in the world?
Best player in the world?
Best CEO in the world?
Best parent in the world?

My guess is you would treat people differently.
My guess is you would use your time differently.
My guess is you would train differently.
My guess is you would take yourself more seriously.
My guess is you would shift your priorities.

Maybe just try it a few times. Ask yourself the question, and then try and operate from that place, rather than operating like you normally do.

It is easy to write off our decisions and play small, but what if we acted like we could be more, even if just for one day?

CHAPTER 43

Fuel

One day my girlfriend at the time asked if I was willing to go completely gluten free. She had noticed that I needed a lot of sleep, and I was getting sick a lot. She thought it was because of what I was eating.

She proposed a deal where she would take care of all the meals for three months, if I would commit to going without gluten.

I reluctantly agreed.

This was incredibly hard at the time, because I was commuting three days a week to train kids and my commute was around 45 minutes each way. Oh, and I was broke. So I couldn't exactly pop into *Whole Foods* to pick up a healthy snack when I needed it.

It was truly amazing what happened.

I felt so much better.
I went from needing 10-12 hours of sleep to needing 6-8 hours of sleep. My energy levels increased dramatically, and I rarely got sick.

If you owned a Ferrari, would you ever skimp and put bad gasoline in it? No! That would be crazy, but so often that's exactly what we do with our bodies.

It's hard to hustle and create if you aren't fueling your Ferrari with premium fuel, and eventually you aren't going to be able to hustle if you don't take care of yourself.

Eventually I started eating a vegetarian diet, though today I eat a pesca-tarian diet. I can't remember the last time I got sick, and I have plenty of energy to do hard, creative work.

Some people say, "I can't afford to eat healthy and shop at places like *Whole Foods*." My response is that, in my opinion, you can't afford not to. Cancer, medical, and doctor bills are much more expensive than eating healthy.

It's really a matter of value, not money. You pay for what you value, and basically you are saying, "I value Starbucks, shoes, Netflix, and going out to eat more than I value my own health." Be honest. Stop lying to yourself and saying you can't afford it. You simply choose not to afford it.

You are going to pay one way or another. I would rather pay for food and save my health, than lose my health and pay for medical bills. Until you fuel your body properly, it will be nearly impossible to hustle with your *best* energy.

Your choice creates your challenge.

CHAPTER 44

Rest

I do not drink caffeine or take any kind of upper, and I do not take any kind of sleep-aid either. From what I have been told, I do something somewhat radical.

I listen to my body.

When I am tired, and it's possible, I sleep. I have created enough margin in my life where this is a possibility, but I have been committed to it for a long time. There are weeks where my body doesn't seem to require as much sleep, and other weeks that it does. I just try and listen.

A lot of people don't listen, and they get sick because of it.

One day I asked my friend Drew Hanlen a question. Drew trains a lot of guys who play in the NBA. I asked him how long the average nap was for a guy before playing in a game that night. His response was, "At least three hours."

I want you to think about this. These are guys with millions of dollars, with people searching the world for the best performance hacks around, but the one thing they can't hack is sleep.

There was a study I read that showed that a college basketball teams field goal percentage increased by around 12% after getting 10 hours of sleep instead of 8 hours.

Hustle is incredibly important, but you also need rest. My advice would be to track how you actually use your time and see where you could trim some excess in order to have margin for rest.

CHAPTER 45

The Story You Create

At some point in my life I realized my story was mine. I realized that the story I told myself about myself matters greatly.

Most importantly, I realized that while I have very little control over what happens to me, I have 100% control over the meaning I give it. It's amazing to me how often people use this narrative to brainwash themselves into believing the worst possible story about themselves.

For example:

"Oh no! It's raining and cold, I always play bad in this weather!"

"Oh no! My best outfit isn't clean for my big day, and I always struggle with my presentations when I don't have on my best outfit."

"Oh no! She is on our team, and we always struggle working with her."

"Oh no! I always struggle when _____."

One of the girls I mentor came up to me before a game and said, "I'm worried because I had a really bad warm up." I looked her right in the eyes and said, "You always play better after a bad warm up." I tell her the same thing when she has a great warm up. "You always play better when you have a great warm up."

Who cares what the scenario is! You have control over the meaning, so why wouldn't you give it the best meaning possible?! No one controls the rules, but you!

You lost a loved one.
You got fired.
Your book got rejected.
Your proposal was shot down.
You got dumped.
Your car broke down.

You get to decide what every one of these experiences mean!

The plot thickens. Awesome! It's *YOUR* story. I love stories like that, and in this story you are the one who gets to determine the meaning, and the meaning you give these events determines whether they are a building block, or quicksand.

Will you write rules that benefit you or constrict you?

The pen is in your hand.

CHAPTER 46

House Cats

I think every young person should become an entrepreneur for at least two years, almost like the mandatory military service that Israel enforces.

Kids would learn so much more running a small business than they do in our babysitting, test-dependent public high schools (and this is no knock on the people serving in schools, who are some of the hardest workers around!). Even Diane Ravitch, the former Secretary of Education responsible for leading the charge in the test, test, test model, now spends her time fighting the monster she helped create.

In the six months between finishing my classwork at Duke and moving out to Los Angeles, I ran a networking marketing business, and I learned innumerable invaluable lessons during that time. I was young, naïve and ignorant. I sold the car I got as my graduation present, and I blew through all that money trying to run this business. In the end, I felt like an utter failure that I let so many of my friends down. Looking back though, I'm so incredibly grateful for that experience, because it taught me that you don't need expenses to run a business and so many more valuable lessons.

It taught me that there is almost always a way to be resourceful and do whatever it is that you think you need to do, but for little to no money. It taught me that there are very few things that will actually give you a strong return on your investment.

From a business perspective, my early failure made me a much more frugal, savvy, and fearless businessman.

Your parents' and grandparents' advice of, *"Go to school, get a good job, buy a house and save some money,"* has become archaic. First off, I don't know how more people didn't go insane on this path, but this path is like a collapsed avalanche area on a ski trail that continues to claim more and more victims. You don't want to go through it. The collapsed trail may not kill you, but if you make it out alive, you aren't ever going to walk the same way.

On top of that, big corporations often unintentionally make people soft like house cats. When you run a bootstrap business, you have to become incredibly lean, resourceful and frugal in order to survive. You learn so much about so many different fields like design, marketing, sales, social media, finance, and many other skills *because you have to.*

It's much different when you aren't putting something on a company card. It's much different when that cost is coming out of your paycheck. It's much different when how you treat that client determines whether or not you'll have any more clients, which determines whether or not you will be able to feed your family.

You can't be wasteful because you don't have anything to waste other than time, but you quickly figure out that time is your most valuable asset.

Many residents of the corporate world are deathly afraid of getting fired, even though I think that in most cases, that's the best thing that could possibly happen to them. Too many people work jobs that they hate, simply because they're afraid of the unknown. They're so afraid of what it would look like if they were forced to move back into their parent's house and blog or build a business from the basement. So, rather than face those fears and chase those lions, they continue to suffer through jobs where they're disengaged, and become mentally overweight.

Nothing has equipped me and helped me become the person of my dreams like running my own business. It requires incessant sacrifice, humility, delayed gratification, boldness, courage, and confidence... daily. All of these are characteristics for which I want to be known.

Here are five principles I've always tried to operate by in my businesses.

1. Provide value to as many strangers as possible. Eventually they will become your clients and friends.
2. Become so good they can't ignore you.
3. Become an opportunist. There is an opportunity in every challenge and problem, so become the person who creates potential solutions.
4. Be bold and courageous enough to fail. So many times I have told really high-level coaches to do something I had no clue would work. Some worked really well, others did not. From those experiments, I was able to figure out a large repertoire of really helpful tools.
5. Your first few hundred iterations will probably suck. Do it anyway.

Even if you stay in a corporate job, make sure you don't turn into a house cat. Operate like an entrepreneur inside of your company, and you will most likely be rewarded with a lot more over which to be faithful.

CHAPTER 47

The Rules Have Changed
(But You're Probably Still
Playing By The Old Ones)

I was on a date with a girl a few years ago, and after explaining what I did to her, she replied (with a perplexed look on her face), "Who qualified you to do this?"

I thought for a second, and then replied, "I did." (No, we didn't have a second date!)

For a second, it looked like her head might explode. Her first thought (along with many others still playing by the old rules) was, "You can't do that!"

Says who?

There's a reason the current epoch of human civilization is called the "Information Age." The internet and social media have given us direct, daily access to the people and the wisdom to which only the elite few used to have access.

The challenge for you and I is that we have to choose ourselves and do the work (hustle). Many times when you try this it feels like you're a fraud. A loud voice in the back of your head keeps screaming, *"You don't belong!"* *"You are a fraud! And everyone is going to find out!"*

Ironically, we think that if we get knighted, that voice will disappear. It won't.

In the last week, I've heard people at the top of their fields in medicine, art, and golf, all tell me that they feel like they don't belong *most of the time*.

One girl told me, "I thought if I could just qualify for the U.S. Amateur tournament, *then* I finally would feel like I belong." But when she did, guess what? *Nothing changed.* I remember still feeling like a fraud, *after* I had been the second outsider to ever work with the greatest dynasty in college sports.

For at least the last hundred years, in order to succeed in life you had to be chosen by an elusive and all-powerful gatekeeper. You were supposed to work really hard, know the right people, dress for the part, then stand in line and hope you got chosen for any job, medical school, law school, sports team, music career, acting, TV show, etc.

The gatekeepers *used* to be the all-powerful decision-makers behind who got the opportunities and who didn't. They were the dream makers and dream crushers.

Five years ago Starbucks, Enterprise, and Target all turned me down for entry-level jobs (thankfully!). But to my benefit and yours, the rules have changed. I didn't have to keep standing in line waiting to be chosen. Let me be clear, the gatekeepers still exist. However, they only wield the amount of power that you give them. You and I have the real power, but we have to choose ourselves, and we have to do the daily, dirty, hard work, and *hustle*, rather than waiting to be knighted by a gatekeeper and told what to do.

This is extremely difficult, because of our psychological conditioning growing up. When we were young, no one needed to tell us to create, learn, and explore. That's just what we did. But, over time, the system beat that out of us with messages like, "Sit down, stand in line, shut up, and *wait* until you're called upon."

116

This conditioning was very helpful for people who worked assembly line jobs, but that era is over, and that conditioning is helpless for the world we live in today.

And don't expect to get much support from friends and family who are playing by the old rules. About three years ago, the person who served as my sport psychologist at Duke was here in L.A., and I took him to lunch. He told me that he thought I needed to go back to school and get my degree in sport psychology. He played by the old rules, so he encouraged me to play by them as well. It's all he knew. He was well-meaning and wanted the best for me, but he was also wrong.

One of the most liberating things that ever happened to me occurred when I moved to Los Angeles, and realized that for the first time I was surrounded by people who were all playing by the new rules. You can play by whatever rules you want, but if you play by the new rules you will make a lot of people mad, and you will no longer have anyone to blame but yourself.

Choose yourself.
Hustle.
Do the work.
Hustle.
Be persistent.
Hustle.
Be patient.

It won't happen quickly, but it *will* happen.

"Robots are the new middle class... Everyone is an entrepreneur. The only skills you need to be an entrepreneur are an ability to fail, an ability to have ideas and to sell those ideas, the courage to execute on those ideas, and to be persistent so even as you fail you learn and move on to the next adventure." — James Altucher

Watch the Gary Vaynerchuk video "6 mins for the next 60 years of your life."

CHAPTER 48

How Much Are You Willing to Suffer?

Friday night after Friday night, Kevin was in the gym working on his game. One night the janitor came up to him and said, "Kevin why don't you ever go out and party with your friends?" Kevin said, "Parties won't take me where I want to go."

You have to be willing to work when others party. You have to be willing to suffer when others play. You have to be willing to do what others won't, so you can do what others can't. It doesn't happen by accident.

Kevin Johnson went on to become an NBA *All Star.*

You can *only* reach your fullest potential by choosing the toughest challenges over and over in life.

How much are you willing to suffer? And I mean really *suffer.*

Because of television, all we see is the glitz and glamour surrounding the lives of very successful people. But we don't see the behind the scenes and the tens of thousands of hours of training, hustling, and grinding they've been doing.

We don't see them getting up before the sun and working long after it goes down. We don't see all the sacrifice and dedication. We didn't see them working when almost no one believed in them.

Everyone has BIG DREAMS, but the best indicator of whether or not you will have a shot, not a guarantee, but just a shot at making your dreams come true, is the truth about how much you are willing to suffer and hustle when no one is watching.

People are often in awe when they hear about the missions Navy Seals are able to pull off, but for years in training they have CHOSEN to undergo egregious and excessive amounts of suffering. *For example, during Hell Week they are only guaranteed 4 hours of sleep during 5 days of excruciatingly difficult physically and mentally demanding work.* Their training is the toughest in the world, but through that pain and suffering some of the greatest warriors in the world are created.

Lil Wayne is a rapper on more songs than almost any other artist, but most people don't know he started writing raps at age eight and that as an eleven-year-old he was writing raps for up to eight hours a day. How many eleven-year-olds, without parental guidance or support, would be willing to "suffer" through that?

We see Kevin Durant's jumper that is wetter than Niagara Falls, and people say he is so talented. But we don't see Kevin Durant in the gym soaked in sweat, intentionally "suffering" three hours before practice starts.

Anyone can dream a dream, but the real question is how much are you willing to suffer. *How many times will you be willing to say NO to instant gratification in order to say YES to your dreams that are so far off they feel like fairy tales?*

How many times will you be willing to persevere in the face of adversity? How many times will you get back up when you get knocked down? How many times will you show up with enthusiasm even though your boss doesn't appreciate your hard work and sacrifice? How many times will you be willing to be called crazy and delusional while you hustle in the dark?

Remember:

First they will ignore you.
Then they will tell you you are crazy.
Then they will tell you are stupid.
Then they will try to sabotage you.
And then, finally, they will ask to borrow your money

If you want to achieve your fullest potential and tap into areas of strength, persistence, and courage you never knew existed, continue to take on the toughest challenges, knowing that your willingness to suffer through the toughest stuff is the greatest predictor of your future success.

CHAPTER 49

What's The Worst Thing That Can Happen?

John Wooden use to say to his guys, "I only have two hundred minutes per game to split between all of you, so I hope that isn't what you are focused on." He went on to tell them that there were an unlimited number of professions that weren't zero sum games, where all the skills they learned from him were applicable.

Sometimes we build in a safety net, and only give half the effort to protect our ego. That way, we always have an excuse. "Well, I didn't even really try!" That might make us feel better in the moment, but down the road it's a very hollow feeling. If I give my everything and I hold nothing back, then I risk my everything not necessarily being good enough, which is an immensely frightening thought. The only way you can truly have no regrets though, is to hold nothing back, be bold, courageous and really go for it.

I don't know about you, but I want to sell out and give my everything. I want to be bold and courageous enough to fail spectacularly! Peter started to sink, but he was also the only Disciple who got to walk on water.

I know that many of the things I'm going to boldly and courageously dive into will not necessarily result in success in terms of results. But if it's not about results, and it's about building my own house, then I will "win" every time.

One question I like to ask people is, "What is the very worst thing that could happen?"

Let's take a golf tournament, for example. You shoot 125? "Oh my God! Yes, that would be the worst thing that could happen." All right, so in your worse case scenario...

Would someone chop off your arm?
Would your parents stop loving you?
Would your friends hate you?
Would you lose your scholarship?
Would you lose your freedoms?
Would you lose access to clean drinking water?

NO!

So if the very worst thing that could happen is your own *embarrassment*, why not be bold and courageous and go for it with absolutely everything you've got?

Why would you play out of fear and try to play it safe?

Playing it safe in life is often the greatest risk of all.

I refuse to believe the key to life is to arrive safely at death. I want to live a bold and courageous life. What is the very worst-case scenario if I start a business instead of taking a safe job or going to school? Bankruptcy? It doesn't work? That's it?

What are we doing? Go for it! *Love attracts energy. Fear consumes it!*

In WWII the English government was nervous because the Germans were threatening to bomb their cities. The English people were overcome with fear, and the government thought it could unravel their entire society.

Then the Germans actually started bombing them, and the craziest thing happened.

Yes, many people tragically died, but those who survived became almost totally fearless in the face of the bombings. Bomb sirens would go off all day long, but rather than cowering in fear, the people developed a resiliency no one could have dreamed of! They just continued on with their lives almost as if nothing had happened.

The Germans would've been much better off had they never actually bombed England and opted instead to let them live in the fear of being bombed. *The fear was much greater than surviving the bombings. The more they bombed, and the more people survived, the more unflappable the English people became.*

After J.K. Rowling was abandoned with her young child and living on welfare, she realized that it wasn't that bad. "Rock bottom became a solid foundation on which I rebuilt my life."

Part of why I think I am so brazen and courageous is because I have lived in a homeless shelter, the closet of a gym, and moved back in with my mom as an adult. I know how to be content with little, so if the worst thing that could happen is I fail, then I'm going to give it everything I've got!

What is the worst thing that could happen if you go for it and pursue that dream in your heart?

If you could die, get burned alive by molten lava, or some other highly tragic calamity, then you probably want to weigh your decision very carefully. But if the worst thing that could happen is you go bankrupt, or experience embarrassment from failure, then why wouldn't you absolutely go for it?

"But Joshua! If I go bankrupt then I can't get a credit card!" So you can't buy things you don't need, with money you don't have, to impress people you don't like? How awful! *You will learn and grow so much more from going for it than you could ever learn from a lifetime of playing it safe.*

It takes the average person who gains a net worth of a million dollars *fifteen ventures* before they hit the million-dollar mark.

123

Build the product.
Start a movement.
Write the book.
Write an article.
Make the video.
Invent that thing.
Become a resource hub.
Learn that skill you always dreamed of.
Solve the problem.

I don't know what your lion is, but I know that you are supposed to chase it.

You don't necessarily need to quit your job and invest all your life savings, but maybe you do. *Ironically, it is harder to be faithful with the smallest version of your dream than it is go out in a ball of fire.* Dream BIG. Think small. What is the smallest version of your dream that you can start today, right where you are, using what you have?

Don't let the fear consume you. The greatest thing that could happen to most of us is that we actually experience the thing we fear and then realize that we're not only still here, but that everything is still okay.

Build it.
Ship it.

It's your turn.
Please take it.
We need you.

Make.
Believe.

CHAPTER 50

You Don't Know Your Why

It's amazing how many people tell you, "You've gotta know your why."

Guess what? Your "why" is probably a lie. We don't know why we do what we do, and how could we? Our brain is processing **eleven million** bits of information per second, and we are only conscious of **forty** of those bits.

Our memories are created through the telling and retelling of stories, rather than the events that took place. I learned all about this studying at Duke University under David Rubin, who is the number two authority in the world on autobiographical memory.

We are constantly bombarded by images, music, stories, videos, and other stimuli every day that impact our choices and decisions in a myriad of ways we are only just starting to understand. We do know that people get paid millions of dollars a year to manipulate and trigger your behaviors in ways that the majority of Americans have no clue about. They think they made a choice, and in theory they did, but truthfully they had very little choice in the matter.

Jeremiah 17:9 says, "The heart is desperately wicked, who can know it?" What does this mean? In my opinion, it means that we have no clue why we do what we do. We might have a guess, but most likely we're just telling a story that sounds good.

You almost never hear, "I work so hard because I'm fearful that if I don't continually prove myself then I will have a hard time believing I am lovable. I spend crazy hours at the office because I despise my wife, and my kids don't listen to me. I work so hard to be able to make as much money as possible because it makes me feel like the god of my own life. I'm trying to become the best in the world because I don't think I'm lovable, and without accomplishments and money I feel worthless. I work so hard and put my babies in day care because I'm afraid of sucking at being a mom and I'd rather stay where I'm comfortable all day, at my job."

It's extremely rare to hear those "why's" articulated from people, but I observe those fears in many people, including the man looking back in the mirror at me.

Like Dale Carnegie said, "There is a reason people tell you, and then there is the real reason."

If I'm being 100% authentically vulnerable with you, I know that much of what drives me is my desire to feel significant and that I never felt unconditional love from my father, which has led me to a lifelong challenge of constantly trying to prove myself through my accomplishments. I have tried to focus on my mission of loving people, serving people and providing value, but ultimately I have no clue why I do what I do.

Quite frankly, I'm tired of hearing people say, "I work so hard to provide for my family, so they can have a life where they want for nothing!"

I went to school with a lot of kids whose families were insanely wealthy, and most of those kids were desperate for love, time, and energy from their parents. Yes, they had incredible experiences and more toys than most, but deep down they wanted and desperately *needed* their parents' energy and love, not their stuff.

I'm tired of hearing about people working tirelessly to build the lives of the people on their team, while their own kids are at home desperate for parental guidance and love while being raised by strangers.

I don't know why I do what I do, so there is no fathomable way I can know why other people do what they do, either. However, what I am very certain about is that knowing our "why" is unknowable, and the "why" often looks like a big lie.

People say all the time, "When you feel like giving up, remember why you started! If you have a big enough '*why*,' you can conquer any '*how*!'" But what if, in conquering the "how," and in your quest for achievement, you're actually sacrificing the things that truly matter in life?

Doubling down on an unwinnable bet is not wise. At some point, we have to put the shovel down.

Francis Chan said, "Our greatest fear should not be of failure. Our greatest fear should be of succeeding at things in life that don't really matter." I don't want to get to the end of my life only to realize that my ladder has been on the wrong building the whole time.

A few small things matter. The rest is virtually meaningless. I hope I'm living my life in a way that lets me maximize the opportunities to impact the few things that will truly matter on my deathbed.

"I thought getting to number one (in the world) was going to be the moment I made sense of my life. But it left me a little empty, and I spiraled down." — Andre Agassi

CHAPTER 51

One Of The Best Pieces Of Advice I Ever Received

I was boiling over with righteous indignation. This person had done something awful, and I was ready to strike back with the brand of vengeance usually reserved for epic Hollywood action scenes starring Liam Neeson.

Just before I hit send on the email, I decided to call my friend Russ. After I explained the situation, he said something very simple yet very profound.

"Joshua, you can do whatever you'd like, but if I were you **I would never leave a voicemail, email, text message, or anything that is recorded that you wouldn't want to be played back or read at** *the worst* **possible time you could ever imagine.**"

Well, that was a real kick in the man-region!

I knew immediately that I should, under no circumstance, send that email. I immediately thought of another piece of advice a mentor from afar had once said:

"You don't lose the right to tell someone off tomorrow, so you should probably just sleep on it today." -Warren Buffett

It's easy and sometimes justified to tell someone off, but I would encourage you to follow Russ's advice. We live in a highly connected world, and something you meant for just one person could quickly be taken out of context and ruin a lot of opportunities for you.

Maybe just take Uncle Warren's advice and *sleep on it.*

CHAPTER 52

Where Do You Want To Be Uncomfortable?

After a hard-fought game that came down to the wire, a woman with a microphone and camera grabbed Brad Stevens and said, "Coach, how does it feel to win such an incredible game like that?"

His response was really interesting. He said, "I don't care about the result, I just care we have no regrets. The pain of discipline isn't as bad as the pain of regret."

I often ask people in workshops and during one-on-one sessions, "Where do you want to be uncomfortable: in training or in competition?" I can guarantee you are going to feel uncomfortable, so the choice is yours as to where you want to feel it.

Is it uncomfortable to use random practice techniques rather than block practice? Absolutely! I hate how annoying it is to change clubs after every shot when I am practicing golf. But I sure loved shooting three under par this summer and breaking seventy for the first time, two months after committing to random practice over block practice.

If you know that you are going to feel uncomfortable at some point, wouldn't you rather feel uncomfortable in training than under the bright lights?

I want to make my training so challenging and uncomfortable that anytime I'm in competition I am comfortable because I've already trained in tougher conditions.

For golf:
- Play once a week with only four clubs.
- Play once a week with someone driving your clubs and run to your ball to hit your next shot
- Only putt into the really small hole during training

For standardized tests like the LSAT:
- Reduce the amount of time during your practice tests by 25%.
- Have people play music, and try to distract you while taking your practice tests
- Take tests in really cold places
- Take tests in really hot places

For sales:
- Ask your most argumentative friend to play the role of customer.
- Try pitching random strangers on the street
- Try giving a practice sales presentation with something in your mouth.

(The Greek orator Demosthenes would practice giving speeches with pebbles in his mouth)

When you flash a random set of words in front of people and ask them to remember and write them down, they don't remember nearly as many as they do when a set of random words are all missing one letter.

The struggle to make sense of that one irregularity forces our brain to remember that set of words better. We need to create impediments for ourselves in order to grow to our potential.

We need to struggle.
We need a challenge.

Where do you want to be uncomfortable?

CHAPTER 53

The Pursuit Of Happiness Is Killing Us

When people fill out our intake forms before workshops and speaking engagements, many times they answer the question, "What is your big dream?" with, "To be happy."

Here is the problem: happiness and fulfillment are oftentimes in direct opposition to one another. *Happiness is about instant gratification.* It is a feeling that seemingly comes and goes. Someone or something can make you happy for a little while, but that feeling can fade and you'll need something new to make you 'happy' once again.

For some people, their pursuit of happiness might come from purchasing new clothes, shoes, or cars. For others, it might be found in having lots of cool friends, travel, or the most beautiful significant other.

Inherent in happiness talk is a strong degree of selfishness. *Happiness is all about me.* How *I* feel. What *I* want.

Another predominant characteristic of happiness is that it is easy. If I have to work really hard for something and put in a lot of blood, sweet, and tears, then I will be sacrificing a lot of short-term happiness, so that is unacceptable. Happiness is supposed to be easy.

The two predominant characteristics of happiness are that it must come easy and it is *me* focused.

Here is the ironic twist. Fulfillment often exists in direct opposition to happiness, because *fulfillment is others-focused rather than me-focused, and it only comes by going through the tough stuff.*

When you ask people in the later stages of life to list the most fulfilling things they've done, they often tell you things like climbing mountains and raising children. When you ask them what were the most challenging things they have done in their life, they tell you things like climbing mountains and raising children.

Over the last one hundred years our "quality of life" has done nothing but climb higher and higher in the United States, yet during that same time so have the amount of people on antidepressants and those taking their own life.

I'm afraid the pursuit of happiness is killing us. Fulfillment is a much deeper and more abiding feeling than short-lived happiness. I fear many people are missing out on fulfillment in the pursuit of happiness.

TRAIN To Be Clutch

- The **BIG LIE** is that satisfaction and fulfillment are found some where higher on the ladder. Happiness and fulfillment often exist in direct opposition to each other. By seeking and pursuing one, we will most likely miss out on the other.
- Happiness is most often *me*-focused and comes through the easy road.
- Fulfillment is most often *others*-focused and comes through the tough challenges.
- Fulfillment is a much deeper and more abiding feeling than short-lived happiness. If you want fulfillment, you most likely have to sacrifice short-term happiness.
- What are some opportunities you have in your life right now where you could shift from, "What can I get?" to, "How can I serve?"
- Who do you know that is a willing servant? What is it like to be around that person?
- What are some things the pursuit of happiness has cost you?

133

CHAPTER 54

Shut Up And Listen

One day I was playing golf with a group of people who coach at a very high level. We worked with two of them, and I believe the other person was very well aware of what we do and the impact we've had on their sport.

On hole three or four I started telling a story to the group, and as soon as I finished, the person we don't work with began trying to argue with me about my points in the story. Maybe I need to grow in this area, but there are very few people I'm going to engage in intellectual debates with, and very rarely is that ever going to happen when I'm enjoying free time on the golf course. I didn't try to debate him, I just made a conscious choice to not share anything else with him. I only shared stories with the guy in my cart from that point on.

If there is one thing I have learned on my journey, it's that the greats know when to sit down, shut up, and listen to people who are wiser than them. I attribute a great deal of who I've become and the success of *Train To Be CLUTCH* to that discipline.

When Judah Smith talks, I have pen and paper in hand, and I'm taking copious notes. If he shares the same talk twice on Wednesday, I stay and take detailed notes for both talks. On the rare occasion he has given the same talk three times, I have stayed and taken notes for all three!

There is a time for debates and asking the hard questions, but there are many more times to sit at the feet of wise people and soak up everything you can. One of the real secrets to success and tapping into your greatness is learning how and when to shut up and simply absorb everything you can.

CHAPTER 55

Living "The Dream" Left Me Depressed

My baby brother drowned when I was nine years old, and I was the one who pulled him out of the pool. My brain was literally scarred, and I know now that I suffered from significant PTSD symptoms after this trauma. Only in the last few years have I been able to piece this all together, and make sense of why I have exhibited manic-depressive symptoms for most of my life.

Interestingly though, over the last couple of years my symptoms have seemingly gotten much, much better. But this summer, that changed; I got really depressed. It was strange because I was living most people's dream life. I had both the money and the time to travel as much as I wanted. I went to Costa Rica twice, spent significant time in Denver, and then visited a few other places in between.

Then, the strangest thing started to happen. *I got depressed.*

Without realizing it, while on the road I had started to stray from my night and morning routine. Every night I listen to a playlist that sows great fuel into my heart, and every morning I sit down in the shower for ten to twenty minutes for a time of focused gratefulness prayer and meditation with Jesus.

Without realizing it, both of those essential habits started to slip badly, and my sleep, moods, and those around me suffered in light of it.

As soon as I got back into my night and morning routine, my symptoms subsided and I was back to more of my normal self. I had subtracted purposeful work and my routines out of my life, and I suffered the consequences because of it.

If you would like to see my playlist, shoot me an email and I'll send it to you! Joshua@traintobeclutch.com

From this experience I learned two really valuable lessons:

1. If you quit on your process (chop wood, carry water), don't be surprised when the results stop showing up.
2. Purposeful work is much more important in my life than I real ized before. Living "the dream" for me is actually doing a lot of things that make a tremendous impact on the world.

My suggestion to you is to make sure you know what routines are greatly enhancing your life and helping you become more of the person you want to become, and also to ensure you define success for yourself rather than letting society do that for you!

CHAPTER 56

Gratefulness Prayer And Meditation

Some of my best and clearest ideas have come from my time alone sitting in the shower in prayer and meditation.

The research is clear that the benefits of meditation are immense, yet most people tell me they can't meditate, that it's too hard. They say they get distracted too easily.

I always suggest gratefulness prayer and meditation sitting in a hot shower, because it is a time when your brain waves slow down and you are already pretty much in a meditative state. I've also found it is a great time to use visualization.

I always start out with gratefulness prayer and just thank God for all the things in my life that are easy to take for granted. Things like clean drinking water, freedom, a bed, food, a hot shower, people that love me, God's scandalous, relentless, and unconditional love, and tools to create. I then *thank* God for all the doors He has closed in my life. If anything is in pain, on or in my body, I take that time to thank God for those muscles, teeth, bones, or organs.

I pray for God's perfect will to be done in my life. Not for things to go well, but for things to go right. For Him to mold and shape my heart into who He wants me to be. For eyes to see people the way He sees them. For everything of Him to pierce hearts and transform minds, and for everything not of Him to drop dead as soon as it leaves my mouth when I speak.

I ask for Jesus to heal my heart, and for me to see myself the way Jesus sees me. I ask for joy, wisdom, and peace to flow like a waterfall over my heart. I pray for Him to help me let go of my insecurities and desire to prove my significance. I ask Him to help me surrender my deepest fears and challenges to Him. I pray to find my significance, identity, and value 100% in Him and being a child of God.

I pray that I would make it more about Him and less about me, and to simply trust in Jesus. I pray for wisdom to articulate simple ideas with reckless love and grace. I pray for people to be encouraged and inspired regardless of whether they come to believe what I believe. I pray to love people like Jesus and that through this love, they would encounter Jesus in me. I ask to become love so that everywhere I go people will want what I have.

I commit everything I am working on, *Train to be CLUTCH*, and my relationship to Him.

At some point I usually just slip into meditation because I unintentionally stop praying and I just sit it silence and let my thoughts go and go. If I have a big event coming up, my mind will often move towards thinking about that workshop or keynote, and I will try to visualize myself delivering it at my very best. I also try and visualize my hot button challenges that tend to set me off or derail me, and I try and see myself overcoming those challenges in controllable ways and focus on the *processes* of doing so.

I then close out almost every morning prayer with, "Not my success, health, or wealth, but your perfect will be done in my life."

CHAPTER 57

Thank You For All The Doors You Have Closed

When she walked into the party wearing those stretchy skin-tight pants that perfectly revealed her J-Lo booty, I was done for. When she decided to dance with me all night, I fell hard for her.

Growing up I was very socially awkward, and I'm sure a lot of people would still consider me so. I would rather participate in an activity than hang out socially. It's typically a rather nerve-racking experience when I walk into a wedding or party and don't know most of the people in attendance.

Needless to say I wasn't exactly a ladies man, especially with braces for three years from eighth through eleventh grade. As if that weren't enough, by the time I was of legal age I'd developed a habit of being a real jerk to most people.

In high school I was made fun of a lot by the other kids who played sports, who made a habit of calling me "gay" every chance they had. The fact that I was probably the best total-sport athlete in the school made little difference, because I only played soccer at high-school. To them, "soccer-fairies," weren't athletes.

Thanks to this, I had a very low self-image and I tried to compensate with arrogance, which as anyone knows does a guy no favors in the lady department. So, when this cutie with a booty started paying attention to me, I fell madly in love. Well, I thought it was love, but it was more likely lust.

Three years later, after a very rocky relationship, I found myself at a crossroads.

I had just given the eulogy at my father's funeral the day before, and it was time to get up for church. That morning, with a lot of prodding, I was able to convince her to get in the shower and finally be away from her phone. My heart didn't have much more room to break, but the forty or so scandalous sexual text messages I found on her phone was my ultimate breaking point.

I was devastated that I had wasted so many years of my life with her. However, if God is who He says He is, and who I believe He is, then it seems strange to me to get frustrated when doors close in my life. Almost every morning I try and thank God for all the doors that close in my life, because no matter how it feels in the moment, I know it's in my best interest.

Looking back today, I'm so grateful I didn't end up married to that girl.
Looking back today, I'm so grateful the homeless shelter didn't put me on salary.
Looking back today, I'm so glad I didn't have my master's to teach at Pepperdine.

There have been so many more closed doors over the years, I've lost count a long time ago. But even though it's always a frustrating thing to endure, I still thank God every time He closes a door, because I know He has my best interest in mind.

141

CHAPTER 58

No Is More Important Than Yes

When I was first starting out, I tried to find a way to say "yes" to every opportunity that came my way, and I prided myself on this.

One day I was talking with one of my mentors, and he said something I didn't understand at the time. He said, "Joshua, over the next few years what you say 'no' to will become much more important than what you say 'yes' to."

I was confused, because I wanted to say "yes" to it all!

Over the last few years, though, I've come to understand the wisdom in what he was telling me. It wasn't too long after that that I was telling Jamie, "I need you to say 'no' to more things."

The thing is, when I say "yes" to something I am also saying "no" to a billion other possibilities. I had to learn that in order to create the necessary time and space to do the hard, creative work, I had to start saying "no" a lot more often. Saying "no" is often very challenging for most people, and a possible beginner step is saying "not yet" instead.

Either way, both do the same job of protecting your most precious resource in the world, your time. And both send the same message to those around you: that your time is valuable, and worthy of protection.

Because the truth is, if you truly want to become great, you must focus on using your time in a way today that pays off in the long run and actually multiplies it tomorrow. And that starts with protecting it.

Will this upset some people? Absolutely!

But will they learn and adjust after you set up healthy boundaries by learning to say "no" and "not yet"? Absolutely!

Jonathan Ive has repeatedly said that the question Steve Jobs asked him every day was, "How many things did you say no to today?" He believed that in order to focus on what truly matters, you need to be saying "no" to almost everything else.

It took me a long time to get it, but saying "no" is one of the most important lessons I've ever learned. **In order to maximize your hustle and your potential, you must learn to say "no" to all the wrong stuff, so that you can finally be able to say "yes" to the right stuff.**

CHAPTER 59

Hustle ≠ Busyness

Some people wear "busyness" like a badge of honor, but let's be crystal clear about something. Hustle and busyness are not the same thing. They may appear similar at first glance, but they are worlds apart. True hustle protects time as the most valuable resource in the world, and uses it only on the most important tasks.

That is probably what made John Wooden issue the warning, "Do not mistake activity for achievement."

I hear people say, "It must be nice to have time to read, but I'm too busy for that."
It's always said in a tone that comes across more like, *"It must be nice to have time to read, but I'm out feeding starving children in Africa, building new wells in Third World countries, and building schools for kids who don't have access to education."*

And if you are Adam Braun or Scott Harrison, who created my two favorite mission driven organizations that tackle those challenges, then by all means I apologize for *making* time to read.

The sad reality is that most people are far from doing those things.

It's like we completely lost sight at some point that we all have *volition.*

You *choose* your schedule everyday.

You *choose* what you will ignore everyday.

You *choose* what you will give your time everyday.

The bottom line is that we make time and give our time to what we value. The problem is, some of us value being busy. It makes us feel good. Studies have even shown it releases dopamine in our brains.

The HARD thing to do is not allow yourself to become infected with the disease of busyness, and actually spend your time doing the work and hustling on the things that matter most: the things that will multiply your time in the future.

Who you become needs to be very high on the list.

The only resource that is the exact same for everyone in the world is time, and how you use what you have today will impact how much or how little you have of it in the future.

Let's stop glorifying busyness.
Let's start putting first things first.

Who and what gets your best energy everyday?

Don't just skim over that...*WHO* and *WHAT* gets your best energy everyday?

You can always make more money, but you can never get more time.

Time is the most valuable resource in the world. Are you investing it or wasting it?

"But I have a mortgage and a job!!"

Well, maybe you could benefit from making some temporary sacrifices (investments) for who you want to become.

145

- Maybe you could move back into your parents' basement to free up resources and time to read and experiment with your passion. (Hustle)
- Maybe it's time to stop treating what you do like a hobby and start becoming deliberate about perfecting your craft. (Hustle)
- Maybe it's time to do a time inventory and see where you ACTUALLY spend your time every week.
- Maybe it's time to tell your boss "no" and your family "yes."
- Maybe it's time to build a better system so you stop having to waste time manually doing things that can be automated. (My biggest challenge!)
- Maybe it's time to start delegating responsibility to those who are waiting for you to trust them.
- Maybe it's time to tell the coffee, sugar, and meat, "no," and your overall energy level, "yes."
- Maybe it's time to give your family less material things and more of your love and energy.
- Maybe it's time to start saying "no" to instant gratification and "yes" to investing in yourself.

Take an assessment of how you spend your time and see how much of it falls under what Sogyal Rinpoche calls "active laziness," using your time on tasks that make you *feel* responsible, but that might be more appropriately labeled, "irresponsibilities."

It's time we stop wearing busyness as a badge of honor and glorifying it as something to be proud of, and instead start making the tough choices to put first things first and make sure our best energy is going into the people and work that matters most.

Hustle and busyness are not the same thing.

It's impossible to become who you want to become if you insist on continually being too busy. Some seasons of your life will be more busy than others, but if busyness has stopped being a season and has become a way of life, then it's time to make some serious changes.

CHAPTER 60

Embrace Chaos

When you become "successful," people want to hear what you have to say and are much more willing to listen to your ideas, but when you're still knee deep in learning how to fall in love with the process of becoming great while hustling in the dark, people often think you're crazy.

In our society we're taught to do many things well, but the challenge inherent in that is if you're good at many things, you've probably mastered none of them. *Education might value balance, but I would argue that our society doesn't.*

When I started to take myself seriously and began reading for twelve hours a day, and spending four more hours on Twitter, many areas of my life erupted with chaos.

Some weeks, I would only shower twice. My room almost always looked like a disaster scene out of the movie *Twister*. I relied heavily on whatever food my mom was making, and sometimes I simply didn't eat much at all. And my car? My car was always filthy! You know what utterly confuses me? People that care more about cleaning out their car than cleaning out their life. Their car will be spotless, yet their life has got all sorts of junk strung out everywhere keeping them from their personal greatness.

What I realized is that it is easier to focus on mundane tasks like cleaning and organizing, than it is to do the tough creative work that greatness requires.

It's easier to clean your room than to write out the ten most valuable lessons you have learned and be vulnerable enough to share them with a hundred people. It's easier to spend time washing and cleaning your car than it is to read a book overflowing with the life-changing wisdom of great people who have gone before you. When I clean my car I get the immediate satisfaction of seeing the finished product, and most importantly *other people* see that. But when I invest in reading a book or focusing on building a system for my business, I might not see a return on that investment for a long time.

I agree with my friend James Clear that our environment greatly shapes our choices. However, I think that in the beginning, too many people use chaos as an excuse to not do the dirty, hard, boring work and hustle.

It's the dirty, hard, boring work that helps us develop our greatness and master our craft. The ironic thing is that if you beat on your craft long enough, if you are willing to sacrifice long enough, if you are willing to embrace the chaos long enough, if you are willing to hustle in the dark for long enough, then you will be able to afford to outsource the mundane tasks to other people so you can keep doing the dirty, hard, boring work.

You shouldn't hve to embrace that type of chaos forever, but you will need to embrace it for a while, especially when you are hustling in the dark.

People in your life might label you as "lazy," "disorganized," etc., but you must understand that you will never become great if you can't embrace chaos.
The greater you become, the more chaos will arrive in different forms. You will have to decipher where your best energy needs to go. I'd argue that your best energy needs to go to the hardest tasks. *Many people are willing to do the mundane tasks, but very few are willing to sacrifice and beat on their craft while chaos ensues.*

"When you strive for greatness, chaos is guaranteed to show up." — Gary Keller

CHAPTER 61

No One Is Original, So Your Best Bet Is To Steal Like An Artist

All great artists start out imitating the greats who came before them, and after they have copied and imitated for thousands of hours, *then*, and only then, do they start to become an original.

I have very little in terms of formal training to do what I do, and although I have a relatively strong grasp on the science of peak performance and psychology, I consider myself more of an artist than a scientist.

When I started out, I relied on two people and one thing: Greg Dale, David Ruben, and my own story. I had taken two classes on performance psychology from Greg Dale, and one autobiographical memory class from David Ruben. Both of them taught at Duke University and were best in class, so when I was starting out I just shared exactly what I learned from them. In fact, I would often reference Greg Dale's slides from our performance psychology class.

After a couple years into this journey, Tony Robbins had a profound impact on my life and teaching, so then it became a combination of those three and my story. Eventually I added Barbara Fredrickson's and Carol Dweck's work, then around six or seven years into my journey of studying, speaking, writing, and mentoring, I finally *started* to find my unique voice.

If you look at all the greats in sports or music, they all do the same thing: they steal like artists. No one is original, so your best chance is to steal like an artist, and then eventually you might find your own unique voice.

"Even in literature and art, no man who bothers about originality will ever be original: whereas if you simply try to tell the truth (without caring twopence how often it has been told before) you will, nine times out of ten, become original without ever having noticed it." -C.S. Lewis

CHAPTER 62

Mirror Neurons

I fly quite a bit every year to different speaking engagements and work-shops, and I've started to notice a trend on flights. *The energy of the person serving as the flight attendant is infectious.*

Whenever I fly *Southwest Airlines*, there is a high probability that my flight crew will serve with big personalities, joy, and care. When I fly other airlines, the opposite tends to happen. I feel like I am just a number, and the person serving would rather gouge out their eyeballs than actually serve us.

The other day I was on a six-hour flight, and the person serving as the flight director made me realize how powerful we can be in each other's lives. This guy was frantic, annoyed, and the more he snapped and got frazzled, the more the people in our area did the same.

The scientific cause for "attitudes and energy are contagious" is called *Mirror Neurons*. We have all these neurons inside of us that tend to mirror the energy and emotions of those around us. That is why we cry in sappy movies, and get a rush of adrenaline when the underdog overcomes a challenge.

Your energy, body language, and self-talk are always affecting everyone around you. (Regardless of whether you, or they, are ever consciously aware of it!)

Toward the end of our flight my girlfriend asked for some water, and the frustrated guy had a very interesting remark. He said, "On this flight everyone asks me for something *before* I have time to serve them!" as he huffed away.

I think that many of us do the same thing every day by blaming our circumstances, our boss, that one person, or something else outside of our control. But the reality is that we are the only ones who can take back control, simply by re-claiming our controllables.

Even when everything is hitting the fan, we can still focus on true mental toughness and things like our attitude, perspective, self-talk, body language, and how we communicate.

If I can be completely honest with you, I think more often than not I am more like the other airlines than Southwest, but I do believe we can all change and grow.

Focus on what matters.
Control what you can control.
Your energy is affecting a lot more than you might have ever imagined.

True Mental Toughness =
Having a GREAT attitude.
Giving your VERY VERY best.
Treating people REALLY REALY well.
Having UNCONDITIONAL gratitude.
Regardless of your circumstances.

CHAPTER 63

Warning:
When You Refuse To Stand In Line And Do What You Are Told, There Are Real Consequences!

Traffic is worse than usual, and I'm already running late to LAX.

Still, I get my bags checked two minutes inside the forty-five minute window, I'm flying first class, and I have TSA pre-check, so I'm not worried.

But as I crest the escalator to approach the security checkpoint, I find crowds of people, packed into multiple lines. I head to the sign for TSA pre-check. Every line is roped off, but there is a clear entry point, so as the line moves forward, I start to merge.

You would have thought I had kicked a child!

Immediately, an elderly not-so-gentle-man tells me, "The line starts back there!" as his delightful life partner begins yelling at me, "You are an entitled kid with a stupid hat! And you are *ugly*!"

I ask them both to please calm down, and tell them that I'm only merging where it seems appropriate, when all of a sudden the elderly man in front of them turns around and says, "You're a jerk!" while trying to crowd me out of the line.

The commotion attracts a vested official, who tells me that I cannot enter the merge line, and that I need to go to the back of another line. I swallow my frustration and inform him that this system is broken, then head to the back of the line he indicated.

When I finally reach the security checkpoint, I'm informed by the TSA officer that I've been randomly assigned to go through their cancer-causing, radiation blasting, full-body scan machine. I calmly reply, "No thank you, I'd much rather be molested by one of your fellow heroes than go through your insta-cancer machine." Okay, truthfully I said, "I'm opting out," but I was definitely thinking that.

Another TSA officer then proceeds to give me the longest pat-down I've ever had, even throwing in an extra rub down along the inside of my leg, gliding up "until I get resistance" (code for, "until I feel your package.")

I've been through this procedure many times while waiting for my TSA pre-check, and while I always feel like I lose a tiny part of my soul, this experience is the closest thing to molestation I'd ever experienced. As this man takes his sweet time feeling me up, I try to distract myself by reflecting on why those people had started to yell at me for merging into their line.

The obvious answer is that they don't like people like me who refuse to wait in long lines, and are always looking for a way to get ahead. But I also think there are deeper implications.

I agree that many people in my generation and our society in general are entitled. And in all honesty, perhaps I am one of them. But perhaps I'm also right in thinking that we deserve a quicker, more efficient, and more pleasant experience when flying.

Like so many other systems in the world around us, it's a broken one.

I think that a lot of people are frustrated that "the system" in life is no longer working for them. Instead, people like myself have figured out that there is another line that goes where everyone wants to go in half the time, and you don't have to get yelled at.

The former gatekeepers are fighting to remain relevant, and the people who played by the rules of the system are incredibly frustrated.

Taxi companies can't believe that clean cars and a pleasant user experience can just show up and erode their business without playing by their old rules.

People can't believe that Social Security isn't paying their bills, or simply isn't going to be around when they retire.

Universities can't believe people in their basements are filming training programs that are diverting dollars away from their "tried and true" methods.

MBA's can't believe that entitled brats like Mark Zuckerberg are qualified to run billion-dollar public companies.

People in the TV world can't believe that a seventeen-year-old with an iPhone has engaged more loyal viewers on YouTube than they have on their primetime shows.People in the music world can't believe that an artist today can use social media, iTunes, and other tools to have a viable career without major label backing.

I would be frustrated too if I had spent my whole life playing by a set of rules that promised a reward, only to watch a group of people who don't play by the same rules get rewarded for it.

There are lots of people in the sport psychology world that I infuriate because I get opportunities to work with people who would never work with them, yet I haven't jumped through the same hoops for their fancy degrees and job titles. *"You can't just say you teach mental training and then go do it! You aren't qualified! You aren't licensed! You have to go stand in line and get yelled at by the lady in the vest just like we all had to!"*

155

My answer is, "Who says?"

There is always a back door to do whatever you want to do, but know that you'll probably get called "ugly" and "entitled" if you choose to use it. You will make a lot of people angry if you choose yourself and build your own back door, but in my experience, it's always been worth it.

CHAPTER 64

Control The Controllables

In life there is very little we have control over, yet when you observe most people, they spend the majority of their time and energy focused on all the things *outside* their control.

This is a quick way to become very miserable.

We address this in our book, *Burn Your Goals*. In it, we said that by focusing on uncontrollable, arbitrary outcome-based goals you decrease confidence, increase pressure, and make yourself miserable in the process.

Now, I'm not Mr. Nice/Super-Positive guy, either. Transformational leadership is not soft or easy, but it also doesn't mean you have to become a jerk or the type of leader for whom nothing is ever good enough. It's just that there is so much *outside* our own control, that we're infinitely better off focusing all our energy on the things *inside* our control.

Here are some examples of things that are *mostly* controllable:

Attitude
Effort
Self-Talk
Visualization
Gratitude
How we treat people
What we focus on

Routine
What we do with our 86,400 seconds every day
What we don't do with our 86,400 seconds every day
Communication
Body Language

Now just to be clear, each of these does have small elements of uncontrollability as well. If a guy gets hit in the "man region," his body language and focus are going to be temporarily outside his control. When a woman is pregnant and in labor, many of those examples may temporarily be 100% uncontrollable. And for some people, natural chemical imbalances can render something as simple as a "change in attitude" a bit trickier than for the rest of us.

However, for the most part you have close to 100% control over those areas.

Rather than focusing on our boss, our co-workers, the market, sales, and other things outside our control, we're much better off to focus on the few things we do have control over. Some people think we are trying to lower the bar by getting rid of goals and focusing on controllables, but we are actually raising the bar.

As you read early, we define *True* Mental Toughness as:

Having a GREAT Attitude.
Giving your Very Very best.
Treating people Really Really well.
Having UNCONDITIONAL gratitude.
REGARDLESS of your circumstances.

The amazing thing about this standard is not only that it is the closest thing to 100% controllable, but when you get fired, are facing a tough challenge, or when things simply seem impossibly hard, all of those scenarios are now an incredible opportunity to develop more true mental toughness.

And guess what?

Everyone wants someone on their team who embodies the characteristics of true mental toughness. So, no longer is it a "bad" thing when you face hardships. No! Instead, it's an incredible opportunity to develop the stuff in life that really matters.

Society, the media, and many well-meaning people will tell you that you must focus your limited energy on things like sales goals, win/loss goals, and other outcomes that are outside your control. But honestly? It's the *process* that drives those results.

More importantly, I want you to develop the stuff that really matters in life. Too many people sacrifice what truly matters at the altar of false success: potentially winning business, or a sale, or a game. Can you focus on outcome-based uncontrollable goals and become "successful?" Yes, without a doubt.

But that doesn't mean you've come close to tapping into your potential. It's not whether it's right or wrong to focus on things outside your control, it's whether or not it's *most beneficial*. Just because you achieved some success doesn't mean you came close to your potential, and I would argue that the only way you're going to become truly successful is to focus on what is controllable and what truly matters.

P.S.: If you want to know what truly matters, just write out your obituary and what you want to be remembered for. Rarely does anyone say anything other than "the impact they had on others" and "who they became as a person." Not even the guy who has won twenty-one national championships wants to be remembered for that.

CHAPTER 65

Expediency

This might seem really silly to you, but when I first started *Train to be CLUTCH*, I was worried about responding *too quickly* to people, because in my mind "important" people were important and thus couldn't respond quickly to you.

That all changed one day when I emailed the guy who has more national championships than anyone will ever win. Anson responded to my email within thirty minutes and my mind almost exploded. Here was a guy who at that point had won twenty national championships, and daily runs the greatest dynasty in college sports, and he is getting back to me that quickly?!

From that day forward, I decided I was going to do my best to respond to people as quickly as possible, whether on Twitter, email, text, or phone calls. Every time Anson gets back to me so quickly, it makes me feel great! Maybe that's a personal problem of mine, but I thought if responding quickly can make people feel better about themselves, then I'm going to commit to being expedient in my responses.

It's not ironic to me that many people tell me that the thing that most impressed them about me was how quickly I always respond to them, and for some people it's one of the reasons they choose to have us work with their organization. Responding to people quickly is simple, but thanks to our over-scheduled lives, it's rarely easy. However, expediency will always be something I value, because I've seen the impact it has had in my life, and in many others.

You may not have a big budget, or as many resources as your competitors, but you do have control over how quickly you respond to people.

At the end of the day, nobody likes to wait.

CHAPTER 66

Footprints Are Easier To Walk In

The other day, I was walking on a desolate and mostly uninhabited beach in one of the most remote places in the world. At certain points, the beach felt more like quicksand than the hard sand beaches near where I live in Los Angeles.

It was exhausting trying to walk in this stuff, but soon I noticed something. When I walked in Steph's footprints, or she walked in mine, we could "drift" off one another. When someone else had already broken through the sand, it was much easier to walk in their footprints. It was still difficult work, especially when we would walk for as far as a few miles through this stuff at a time, but overall it became infinitely more doable.

When I first noticed how much easier it was, I mentioned it to Steph. She can be very independent and strong-willed and she kind of brushed me off.

But what I noticed after we both were exhausted from walking, is that she had started to walk in my footsteps. And on our return journey, we *both* tried to walk in our original footsteps from the first half of our trip.

Walking through the quicksand got me thinking about life.

One day, my friend Judah Smith was sharing with a group of people about how God has already gone before us, and He knows everything we are going to do. Not only did and does He know it, but He loved us so much in spite of all the bad and stupid things we are going to do that He chose to sacrifice His only son on a cross so that we might have freedom, life apart from sin, and most importantly, a personal relationship and fellowship with Him.

I think that a story about one of Jesus' closest disciples exemplifies this idea. Most of Jesus' Disciples were teenagers, except for this guy named Peter. He was closer to twenty-one years old, and Peter gets a lot of the airtime in the New Testament. At the last supper, Jesus tells His Disciples that one of them is going to betray Him. Peter, kind of like myself, had a propensity to open his big mouth at the wrong time. Peter emphatically tells Jesus that under no circumstance would he ever deny Him.

But Jesus has gone before, and He isn't bound by time in the way you and I are, so He already knew that later that night Peter would deny Jesus three times, one of which would be to a middle school girl. (In Peter's defense, I've met some very cruel middle school girls!)

Why would Jesus tell Peter that he was going to deny Him three times?

Why would Jesus rub that in his face?

Judah argued, and I would agree, that the main reason Jesus told Peter was because He wanted him (and us) to know, "I've already gone before you. I've always known what you were going to do, and I chose to love you, and will continue to recklessly love you in spite of yourself."

There is an incredible verse in the Bible that says, "For we are God's handiwork, created in Christ Jesus to do good works, which God prepared in advance for us to do."

I LOVE that!!

God already has gone before me.
God has already gone before you.

He has created the footprints for us to walk in, and you and I can drift off of Him. He has made a path for us. He promises that He will never leave us or forsake us.

He doesn't say it will be easy, that storms won't come, or that we will understand all the craziness of this world, or our fickle human nature. But He does promise that He has been before us, that He will never stop extravagantly loving us, and that He will always be with us.

CHAPTER 67

Hot Tub

As we walked back to my apartment, I asked her if she had a good time. She said, "Yes, those girls were really nice!" Somewhat confused, I asked, "Aren't most girls really nice?" Her face tightened and her head started shaking as she replied, "Oh no! *Most* girls are really catty!" At that point I immediately switched from date mode to teaching mode (which is very possibly why I stayed single for such a long time!) ☺

I asked her, "Would you agree that these girls are *not* catty in at least one area of their lives?" She paused and reluctantly said, "Yes, I'm sure in at least *one* area of their lives they aren't catty." I said, "Cool, so that means that they aren't robots, and that you play a role in the interaction. And if you believe that girls are catty, then you will subconsciously or consciously do things to bring that behavior out of them. Unknowingly you have created a vested interest in the situation so that you can then say, 'See! Girls are catty!'"

For some strange reason, we never had a second date

You and I do this same thing, all day long, with different things and different people. We carry our beliefs about the world and about people in our worlds, and those beliefs shape the world we create, attract, and repel around us.

In any given second, our brain is processing around 11 million bits of information, yet our conscious brain is only aware of around 40 of those bits. *In other words, our brain blocks out 99.9999% of what it is process-ing, this doesn't even include everything else that is happening around us.* What determines that .0000364% that we are conscious of? *Our beliefs.*

So, what you *see* might feel like 99% of the picture but it might actually be less than .0001% of what is *actually* happening.

Try this exercise:

Fill in the blank with the first word the pops in your mind.   Be honest.

Life is _____?
People are _____?
Men are _____?
Women are _____?
Business is _____?
Reading is _____?
Eating healthy is _____?
Exercising is _____?

The first word that pops into your mind is a pretty good indicator of your belief. To me, it's not a matter of whether your beliefs are right or wrong. Rather, it's a matter of whether or not your beliefs are the most beneficial ones you can hold for your life.

Now, I would highly encourage you to take it one step further and list seven to ten people you spend the most time around. Try and think of at least two people who are in positions of authority over you, at least two people who are in positions serving under you, and at least two people you are in close relationship with.

It should look something like this:

Sarah is _____?
Jamie is _____?
Mike is _____?

Once again, be honest with yourself and write out the first word that pops into your mind. When you look at this list, are those beliefs the most beneficial beliefs you can hold about those people? In what ways could you be unknowingly contributing to bringing that behavior out of them?

I did this exercise once in Tulsa, Oklahoma and one of my childhood best friends was there. Afterward, he told me that his wife, Lindsey, never sees the bad in people. I told him I called people like that *delusional* and that he might have been missing the point of the exercise. He said, "No! She never sees the bad in people because she always brings out the best in everyone. It's crazy! She believes so much in people that she always brings out the best in them."

I was blown away.

I don't know about you, but I want to become the type of person that brings about the best in everyone I come across. One way you can start to work on that is to take out a clean sheet of paper and do the exercise again, but this time write out what you want to bring out in all those people. I would re-write that new belief about them every day for the next 30 days, and try to catch yourself every time you slip back into the old belief.

Eventually, if you sow some new beliefs in your heart for long enough, you might be surprised at what you start to create, attract, and repel in the world around you.

CHAPTER 68

Stop Just Thinking Outside The Box

Instead, start habitually *acting* and *experimenting* outside the box.

Treat people like people.
Move to another city.
Sell all your stuff.
Move to a foreign country.
Quit your job.
Become a consummate experimenter.
Chase the stuff that scares you.

Most of the things I did scared the life out of me before I did them.

Speak in front of thousands of people? (I can be super shy and introverted)
Move to one of the biggest cities in the world where I know no one?!
Move into a homeless shelter? (Skipping scholarships to law school and not writing my masters thesis from Duke will be a huge regret)
Move into the closet of a gym? (That just sounds crazy)
Create the first mental training apps in the world for basketball, soccer, and golf? (You have no money and no tech background)
Share mental training tools and ideas with people at the top of their craft? (You don't even have a psychology degree)
Write a book? (Who will read it? You don't have a publisher!)

On the other side of the fear, people tell you how amazing it is and how inspiring you are, but in the midst of the journey you feel like you're pooping your pants in public wearing nothing but your tighty-whities!!

But the thing is, it's not about thinking or the idea. Everyone has great ideas. The thing that most people can't or won't do, is to habitually, repeatedly and consistently *act, fail, and learn* outside the box.

It's not an accident and it's not luck. It is habitual and deliberate passion, persistence, hustle, and patience in **ACTING** *outside the box. They will call you crazy and delusional when you start. Then they will call you talented and lucky when you get to do the things they can't because you were willing to habitually do what they would not.*

"Anyone who dreams of an uncommon life eventually discovers there is no choice but to seek an uncommon approach to living it." — Gary Keller

CHAPTER 69

Just Care

It's amazing how often people tell us the thing that sets *Train to be CLUTCH* apart is that, "You actually *care*."

It's funny to me, because it's such a simple thing. But simple rarely means easy.

After I speak, I do my best to be fully present, kind and compassionate toward every single person that comes up to talk to me. I know what it's like to want to talk to the person who spoke and how it feels to get treated like you don't really matter. It sucks! I also know what it's like to go up and talk with Judah Smith after he preaches, and even though he sometimes literally has a hundred people waiting to speak with him, he looks you in the eye and patiently talks with you as if you are the only person in the room.

I don't tell you this to brag about us, I tell you because of the impact it has on people and how few people actually do it (I know I struggle with it at times as well.)

Just *care*! It will set you apart from the rest.

And please don't ever use the trite, flawed logic of, "It's business, not personal." At the other end of your business are people, and people have feelings. Treat them with care, respect, and like human beings, and they will love you and sing your praises everywhere they go. Do the opposite, and your customers will soon migrate to a "business" that actually cares.

CHAPTER 70

If You Are Honest, This Is Probably Your Biggest Addiction

"What is the biggest addiction in the United States?" Tony Robbins asked. I started racking my brain...

Food?
Alcohol?
Drugs?
TV?
Social Media?

Man! As I thought about my list, I felt like it could be any of them. But his response surprised me...

"Problems," he said. "Problems are the biggest addiction in our society. We meet our needs through our problems." My mind was blown, and there was a part of me that didn't really believe him. Then I started paying more attention to people around me.

In which direction did almost *every* conversation go?

"My boss is such a jerk."
"Can you believe that she would say that about you?"
"Ugh, can you believe we have to meet at that time?"

"My kids won't sleep through nap time."
"Oh you think that is bad? Let me tell you about my husband/wife/boss/teacher/coach!"

When I started to become more aware, it became painfully obvious that Tony is right: **problems are our society's biggest addiction.**

I started asking people, "What was the best part of your day?" Try it yourself, especially right when your friend starts in with, "You won't believe the day that I had…"

One day I was having a conversation with a friend of mine who worked a very dangerous job for fourteen hours a day, six days a week. I asked, "If you were to go get a beer with one of your coworkers after work, what would you talk about?"

I asked him right after he told me how demanding and stressful his job was. He said, "We would probably talk about our problems at work." "On your free time?" I asked, and he chuckled and admitted it didn't make much sense. I told him not to feel bad because most people do the exact same thing.

If you want to become wildly successful, stop focusing on problems and become known as a consummate experimenter with solutions. Focusing on problems only makes us unable to see and create potential solutions. In his incredible book It's Not About the Shark, David Niven writes about a really interesting study. In this study, they found that engineers who were shown a design with problems were up to seventeen times more likely to fail to create a design that solved the problem than those who just created a design without ever seeing the problem.

Focusing on, talking about and becoming addicted to our problems might make us feel strangely good in the moment, but it almost completely inhibits our ability to create solutions. **If you fight the need to focus on the problems in your life, you might realize – just like Steven Spielberg did after blowing his entire budget on a mechanical shark that didn't work –** *that it's not about the shark.*

CHAPTER 71

Pure Manipulation

One of the toughest realizations I had to come to grips with in my life was that almost everything I did was to manipulate people and results. It was some time after reading the book *How to Stop the Pain* that I realized I did almost nothing based on who I was, and almost everything based on what I could get, or hoped to get, or how other people treated me. Let me tell you, it set me up for a world of frustration and heartache.

When it came to beautiful girls, I did all sorts of things for them, and even tried to be incredibly sweet and romantic, but that's not necessarily who I was. It was just what I did to try to get them to love me.

When it came to pursuing new friendships, I bent over backwards and did anything for those I wanted to be in relationship with, because I wanted them to love me. I didn't think I was lovable if I didn't do those things.

When it came to sports, I worked really hard and gave my everything, not because it's who I was, but because I wanted to win. If I worked that hard and lost, I was bitter and angry that I had wasted my time.

The saddest thing to me is that I hear this type of behavior promoted all the time. "What is your end goal? What is the outcome you hope to achieve? Once we know that, now we can work backwards to come up with all the things that we can do in order to manipulate the world to give us what we want!" (Okay, I added that little twist on the end!)

Rarely, or better yet never, do I hear people ask, "Who are you? Who do you want to become?" That is what I'm very interested in. It's easy to love people, be kind, treat others well, be grateful, work hard, and give our best when the goal is in sight and we think we can reach it. It's easy when we are interacting with kind, considerate, and amazing people.

What I'm more interested in is what you are going to do when no one is watching, and the goal is completely out of reach?

What are you going to do when you get cheated on?
What are you going to do when your coach doesn't treat you fairly?
What are you going to do when you get fired?
What are you going to do when people take advantage of you?
What are you going to do and who are you committed to being when everything is hitting the fan?

Stop trying to manipulate. Do what you do because of who you are. What would you do if you knew you would get nothing in return, or if you knew all your hard work wouldn't end in a promotion, a raise, a championship, or the relationship of your dreams?

Let go of the expectations.
It's about you, and who you want to become.
Surrender the outcome.
Fall in love with the process of becoming great.

CHAPTER 72

Observing vs. Judging

I have an awful confession to make. When I was really young, my dad would take my brothers and I to public places and we would judge people based on their weight. We used names like, "Big Mac Club," the "Double Big Mac Club," and the "Triple Big Mac Club."

This is horrible, and I feel awful about it… but it happened.

It also ingrained in me, from a young age, a tendency to constantly judge people everywhere I went, and consequently to constantly judge myself as well. Add to that the fact that we live in one of the most judgmental societies of all time, and it was a true recipe for creating massive amounts of emotional pain in my life.

A question I like to ask people: is it illegal to kill someone in the United States? Most people tell me emphatically, "Yes!" The truth is "it depends."

What does it depend on? Well, judgment.

In some cases we actually celebrate the act of killing people in our society. Police kill people. George Zimmerman killed a kid and was judged innocent of committing any crime. The military kills people every day, and many of those kills are celebrated.

I'm not here to debate whether this is right or wrong. I'm just letting you know that it isn't necessarily illegal to kill people in this country. It depends on judgment.

Our whole society is based this way, and I think this is a very slippery slope for us. If you believe that the Bible is the word of God, then before the fall of man in the Garden of Eden, judgment between good and evil is actually the only thing humanity did not have. One could argue, it is the one thing we were not created with a capacity for. I can use my iPhone as a hammer, but that's not what it was created for, and it is going to take a serious toll on it if I do.

Therefore, any time we engage in judging, we increase the likelihood of emotional pain. For the first twenty-three years of my life, before I read How To Stop The Pain, I was often called a "drama queen." I was constantly wrapped up in judgment and judging why everyone did anything and it created all sorts of emotional pain for me. **I thought other people were the ones inflicting the pain because of what they did, but in reality, no one holds that power but me. It was actually the judgment and significance I gave their actions that had the power over me.**

I'll often ask young women in workshops, "If a person living on the street said that you were a lying slut who was going to burn in hell, would that affect you that much?" Most of the time they tell me it would have little effect on their day (because they judge the person and the interaction as pretty meaningless and the person as probably crazy).

But then I ask them, "What if your mom or dad said the exact same thing to you?"

Their facial expressions completely change and they admit this would greatly impact them and would be incredibly painful, possibly even debilitating, moving forward. The interesting thing is that in both scenarios the exact same thing happened to them, but the difference is in the first they judged the interaction as meaningless, while in the other they judged it as incredibly meaningful. What this means is that the power rests in your hands to determine whether something is emotionally painful or not.

You can't believe the number of times I sit down with people and they pour their hearts out to me, sharing all the times they have been emotionally hurt by others. The sad part is they are actually the ones with the power. Eleanor Roosevelt once said, "No one can make me feel inferior without my permission," and I would amend that with, "No one can emotionally hurt you without your permission, either." It is your own judgment that actually creates the emotional pain, not the other person's. In effect, the other person is actually powerless, just like the person living on the street. You and I are the ones with the power.

One of the most powerful things we can do to release ourselves from emotional pain is to take back control, and learn to observe rather than to judge.

My counselor growing up taught me the *51% principle*. In business, if someone owns 51%, then they control the business. In life, that means I need to make sure I have at least 51% control of my own life at all times. If someone else's action has control over my emotions, then I need to take a step back and realize I have over-invested and I need to take back at least 51%. The other thing I must learn to do is to observe rather than judge.

Observing is taking stock of *what* a person did, not who they are, or *why* they did it. One of the quickest ways to know whether I am judging is my use of the words, "because" or "_____ is."

"She cheated on me because I wasn't giving her the emotional support that she needed." "*He is* a jerk." "*She is* a witch."

A few examples of observing would be: "When I was out of town, he cheated on me." "My boss demoted me."

As soon as I start to describe "why," "because," or place a label on the person, I have crossed the observation line and entered into judgment. Observing is merely taking note of the objective facts of the situation.

I released myself from vast amounts of emotional pain when I stopped judging everyone and everything, and instead started setting up healthy boundaries based on people's track records. If we don't set boundaries, then we instead set ourselves up for emotional pain on either side of the coin. If I judge someone to be a "great guy" or a "jerk," then I am setting up blinders to that person's actual track record. I need to simply observe their track record, and set up boundaries based on it.

The greatest indicator of future behavior is past behavior, so by observing track records I can set up healthy boundaries to hopefully create a healthier relationship based on a track record, not on judgment. The simplest way to think about observing versus judging is this: create healthy boundaries based on people's actions, not their words.

People with poor track records love to tell you all the reasons you should not look at their track record and, instead, judge their heart. You will often hear them refer to themselves and others as "good," "bad," or some other type of judgment. It feels good to listen to stories, and sometimes they sound amazing, but you will avoid incredible pain if you stop listening and start observing.

The Bible says the heart is desperately wicked, who can know it. And the fact that we're only aware of .00000364 of what our brain is processing any given second doesn't help. We have no clue why we do what we do, much less why someone else does what they do.

It might meet some of our needs or make us feel better to try and figure out all the "why's" in the world, but it creates an avalanche of emotional pain in the process, and we usually only discover a sliver of what is actually going on anyway.

The healthiest and most beneficial way to free yourself from emotional pain and heartache is to observe people's track records and then create and enforce healthy boundaries with love and respect.

People can change.
People do change.
Don't take their word.
Observe their track record.

CHAPTER 73

Let's Get Weird

Jamie always says it's helpful for me "get weird" with groups, but I'm not sure if this is exactly what he had in mind. Nevertheless, here I go…

Allow me to be completely and embarrassingly vulnerable with you. When I was in junior high I was slightly concerned (okay, more like obsessively insecure) with how my pant-wear lay around my "man area."

No joke.

I would constantly check and see how different pants/shorts made my "bulge" look.

Yes, I'm serious.

Please stop laughing. This is painful for me to recall. I would agonize over this for days at a time. I can't recall what I was supposed to learn in geometry, but I can vividly remember which pants made my bulge look good, and which pants made me want to go cry in the corner. What made it worse was that I attended schools that had a dress code in junior high, and so there were days when I was completely mortified over this issue and there was little to do but hide when my "good" pants were dirty.

We all know that comparison is the thief of all joy, and as a big kid this is still very challenging for me, not to mention when I was thirteen years old. The worst was gym class. This is ironic, because I was always one of the most athletic kids at every school I attended. I was the only seventh-grader to ever start for the junior high basketball team, and I had a green light anywhere in the gym. On the high school varsity soccer team, I started as a seventh-grader as well. But the thing about gym class is that we had these thin, tiny grey shorts that were made out of t-shirt material we had to wear.

Not only was I obsessed with how my "bulge" looked, I was obsessed with comparing how mine looked to the other boys. One day I made the mistake of looking to my left as we lay down to do an exercise, and Nathan, who was only in sixth grade, had a bulge that could make an adult film star jealous. I think I had about three hairs under my arms at this point, and in the thin shorts my bulge basically caved inward. It was bad enough that I was focused on my own pants, but after seeing Nathan that day, I thought my life was over. I was certain, *I am never going to be able to find a wife.*

So, what's the point of all this? *What I've come to realize is that many things that feel like they matter greatly in the moment, don't really matter at all.* Not in the grand scheme of things, anyway. In my experience, often what feels like it matters greatly in the moment matters very little as soon as I gain *perspective*. The challenge is, how can you create perspective in the moment?

Here are some of the things I've found that help me regain perspective.

- Reminding myself of people that have NOMA because they don't have access to clean drinking water. So, I say to myself, "At least I have access to clean drinking water."
- Spending time with or seeing a picture of my brother Luke.
- Listening to a Judah Smith talk.
- Doing a gratefulness walk.
- Reading a great book.

Chances are, whatever I'm worried about or insecure about right now is going to seem as silly as worrying about how my pants lay over my man-area a few years from now (or even just a few weeks or days from now).

Find things that help you regain a healthy perspective and it will not only add years to your life, but it will greatly increase the joy and experience of those you do have.

CHAPTER 74

Inner Child vs. Inner Perfectionist

When I was young, I used to make these drawings with markers where I would take around five different markers at a time and just color a page simultaneously with all of them. Many people thought it was just scribbling, but I thought it was art. I thought it was beautiful and incredible.

As I moved into my teenage years, I came to believe that I wasn't creative because I couldn't draw well. I don't know if this was mostly my own self-sabotage or just my environment, but I do know that it was real. I gradually became hyper-aware that my art wasn't good, and that other kids' art was.

Eventually I stopped drawing altogether, believing that I simply couldn't draw. I had learned to suppress my inner child that wanted to create, design, and act outside the box, because I was afraid of my inner perfectionist.

A research study recently found that I'm not an anomaly when it comes to this. If you ask a kindergarten class, "If you are an artist, will you please raise your hand?" almost every hand will shoot up. But by sixth grade, only one or two brave souls still believe that about themselves and are willing to raise their hands. That is what led Sir Ken Robinson to say that our education system "kills creativity."

I think that both an inner child and an inner perfectionist lives inside each of us. I think both of these personalities can play vital roles in the development of ideas, but that you must know the order they ought to operate in for optimal success.

Perfectionism is much more of a debilitating cancer that crushes more projects and dreams than it benefits. Sometimes, it can be very useful, and helpful in aiding a person or project reach their greatest potential, but often times those who suffer from "perfectionism" are battling very dark demons that are all too perfect at ridiculing their every flaw and making them feel personally worthless.

My father was a perfectionist. It made him a brilliant eye surgeon, but an awful dad to me most of the time. I have lost many friends and burned many bridges because of the perfectionist gene I battle inside of myself as well.

To be quite honest, perfectionism, scares the heck out of me because it is a greater reflection of me then it is of what I see.

At the end of the day, I want people to become the greatest version of themselves, but if I don't make them feel loved and valued in that process then it is self-defeating.

At the end of the day, I want to become the greatest version of myself, but I also know that is impossible if my inner perfectionist is the one who is allowed to run my life.

For me, I know that I *must* allow my inner child vast spaces to run and play, to freely think, create, and act. Thankfully, when I moved to Los Angeles in 2009, I was surrounded by people who did just that.

The temptation in our hypercritical, hyper judgmental society is to let your inner perfectionist run your life, but this is deadly. If perfection is what you seek, then even getting started, or ever creating something good enough to share, is all but impossible.

I try and let my inner child create create create, and then I often share that work with a few people I trust, and they help clean it up and make it better. Then I try and publish it, knowing full well that it has flaws. *This drives my inner perfectionist crazy.* But honestly, I've allowed my inner child the space and freedom to tell my inner perfectionist to shut up and sit in the corner. My inner child is in charge, and quite frankly is doing a much better job at running this area of my life than my inner perfectionist ever did.

Only after something has been published do I let the inner perfectionist have some room to operate and look at everything with a critical eye for how it can be better. The beauty of it is that once I've shared it with the world, then I have the opportunity to receive real-world feedback to drown out the inner perfectionist's hollow voice that says, "No one will benefit from this imperfect mess!"

For too long, my inner perfectionist was given free reign to terrorize and cage my inner child's creativity and unique way of seeing the world, but thankfully today I believe the balance is much better.

Who will you allow to run your life: your inner child, or your inner perfectionist?

CHAPTER 75

The Mask You Live In

I was sitting in class at Duke, and something was different. For most of my life, classes had rarely held my attention, but this time I couldn't turn away. Why?

Greg Dale was teaching this class and it was about sport psychology.

He was sharing about how some people have an alter ego that they use to play inside of. This alter ego often goes by another name, and has very different characteristics than their "normal" personality.

He went on to explain that some people try and see themselves as a "superstar" in their sport, and that they have some type of trigger that shifts them into a different personality. For example, a person might trigger their personality shift to Michael Jordan or Peyton Manning when they pull on their jersey. For others the trigger might be hearing a song, or crossing a certain line on the court or field.

Meanwhile, I was thinking, *this is quite possibly the stupidest thing I've ever heard! Are you kidding me? An alter ego?!* Then all of a sudden it hit me...

Joshua, your whole life has been an alter ego.

Growing up, my family lived in Chicago, and so of course one of the first things I ever said was, "Go Bears," (pronounced more like "dough bears.") My family nicknamed me "Bear" and it stuck, especially in sports. The older I got, and the more competitive the sports got, the more I became "Bear" on and *off* the field.

As I sat there in class, I decided it was time to shed that name. I realized "Bear" was the mask I lived in. I got myself into so many disturbing situations on and off the field, and so much of it was linked back to the mask I lived in.

That season at Duke was the first time I didn't get a single red or yellow card in my entire four-year career in collegiate soccer. Many people who knew me were more shocked that I got no cards that year than they were that I was named the *Duke Student Athlete of the Week, the ACC Player of the Week,* and finished second in points on the team that year to the best player in the country.

Fast-forward three years, and I was sitting in a Tony Robbins seminar when he asked this question: "Which personality runs your life and what is their name?"

Tony went on to explain that most people have at least three different personalities and each of them has different names. I watched as he helped a young woman identify which personality was running her life, and how it had come about as a defense mechanism to pain she had experienced as a child, and how it was actually inhibiting her from becoming the best version of herself.

I realized Joshua Michael Medcalf was the best and most authentic version of myself, and I started asking people in my life to refer to me as Joshua instead of Bear.

Names are powerful, and sometimes can change the trajectory of your life.

In the Bible, there were many name changes, and I think it is because of how powerful names are.

What mask have you been living in?

I would challenge you to think carefully about the nicknames and names you use for others and that they use for you. *You may think those names are playful and innocent, but many times that mask is a prison someone is living in.*

CHAPTER 76

Do It Anyway

Can I be authentically vulnerable with you?

I wasn't ready.
I have never been fully prepared.
I have always been in over my head.

Vanderbilt. (22 on my ACT)
Duke. (Didn't even start at Vanderbilt, now playing on #1 team in the country)
The homeless shelter in a city where I knew no one.
Starting a nonprofit.
Creating the first mental training apps in the world for basketball, soccer, and golf. (No sport psychology degree)
Giving my first keynote to a thousand people.
Being the director of mental training for UCLA women's basketball. (No sport psychology degree)
Writing a book. (C's in almost every writing class)
Mentoring people in coaching with 20+ years experience. (Only coached nine-year-olds for one year)
Doing workshops with professional sports teams. (Never played professional sports)
Hosting our own retreats.

I have never been ready or prepared, but one thing I've learned on my journey of falling in love with the process of becoming great is that you are never truly ready.

The only way you get prepared and ready is by actually experiencing the thing you are afraid of doing, but that you know in your gut you are supposed to do.

The timing will *never* be right. There is no such thing as perfect timing. Do me a favor and turn your "What if's" to "Even if's."

What if this fails?
What if no one purchases it?
What if I'm not good enough?

Even if this fails...
Even if no one purchases it...
Even if I'm not good enough... (yet)

Start to see your life as a story, and remember that every great story has plot twists, trials and hardships. We love stories where the unlikely hero overcomes adversity and chooses to act in spite of facing seemingly impossible odds. What is the worst thing that can happen if you approach it with a growth mindset? You gain invaluable experience; you learn and grow.

Something corrodes and dies inside of you when you refuse to live your mission and purpose in order to play it safe. You weren't created to play it safe. The greatest risk of all is playing it safe, and I refuse to believe the purpose of life is to arrive safely at death.

YOU are the unlikely hero.

The fear will always be there.
Do it anyway.

The lack of resources is real.
Do it anyway.

The lack of experience might set you back.
Do it anyway.

189

YOU are the unlikely hero.
Do it anyway.

"The greats weren't great because at birth they could paint, the greats were great because they paint a lot." — *Macklemore & Ryan Lewis 'Ten Thousand Hours'*

CHAPTER 77

Get It In The Air

"It takes an incredible amount of time, energy, and resources to get your plane in the air," said Loral Langemeier to all the people at her free business seminar in Dallas, Texas. I was only twenty-three years old as I sat in the audience listening to her, but I have never forgotten the lesson. She went on to talk about how you could change planes once you got in the air, but first you needed to get your plane in the air, and most people quit before that happens.

Once I moved to Los Angeles, I saw it all the time. People would move from one big idea and opportunity to the next, and they would never spend enough time or energy on one idea to actually get their plane in the air.

I often tell one of my childhood best friends, "Wash dogs and walk windows." Sometimes I even tell her to, "Walk dogs and wash windows."

I think too often people get caught up in a **BIG** dream, and they aren't willing to just be faithful and hustle with something really small to get their plane in the air. Do you know how many entrepreneurial lessons you would learn if you were committed to walking dogs and washing windows? Then, you can leverage that wisdom (and cash flow) into moving on to something that *is* closer to your dream world.

I'm not against starting on your dream by any means, but sometimes, in some situations, that is close to impossible. However, I've never met someone who couldn't walk dogs and wash windows in their spare time. The issue is most people just aren't *willing* to do something like this.

Entrepreneurial runways all over the world are full of abandoned planes that crashed at the end of the runway. Planes that would have made it in the air if the pilot would have hung in there just a little bit longer, but right when things got really tough (planes do take off against the wind) they abandoned their plane for another plane. Sadly, they then have to go back and start at the beginning of the runway to get the next plane in the air.

Be faithful with whatever opportunities you do have, and be committed to getting your plane in the air. Maybe your plane is a two-seater prop plane that's busted up and ugly, but in the land of dreams it is ironically much easier to upgrade in the air than on the ground.

You will be hard-pressed to get people to give you a sleek luxury jet if you've never gotten a single plane into the air.

CHAPTER 78

Consistency Is Sexy

Consistency in the midst of the storms and mountaintops is one of the most powerful, sexy, and beneficial things you can train.

To some people this comes much more naturally *Jamie Gilbert!

You are probably awesome at consistency as well, but if I can be authentically vulnerable with you, consistency is one of my biggest struggles. If we are all really honest though, everyone of us are consistent. The real question is what are you consistent at?

Do you consistently hustle?
Do you consistently make the world a better place?
Do you consistently *Chop Wood Carry Water*?
Do you consistently bring out the best in those around you?
Do you consistently live by our principles instead of your feelings?
Do you consistently bring out the worst in those around you?

My dad struggled immensely with consistency in raising me. He was incredibly hard on me, and completely soft on my brother. I never knew what to expect from my dad. His reactions to me were very bi-polar, sometimes I could get grounded for months at a time, and other times I would be congratulated for something similar.

My younger brother would probably say I treated him very similar to how my dad treated me. As I mentioned earlier, my family nicknamed me

Bear" when we were living in Chicago and my mom always said it was the perfect name for me because I could either be a Grizzly Bear or a Teddy Bear.

When I was playing soccer in college people would come to games in part just to see what crazy things I would do. Sometimes it was a brilliant goal or assist, other times it was ninja tackling someone and starting a brawl, yelling at our head coach, or many other selfish antics. My coaches were always frustrated because I lacked beneficial consistency.

For the first 25 years of my life, I was consistently inconsistent.

Over the last 5 years I have trained very intentionally to create more beneficial consistency in my life. I don't like structure, but I have found that when I create some structure and consistency I have really enjoyed the fruits of my labor.

I have found that when I consistently start my day in gratefulness prayer and meditation, it goes much better. I have more clarity, patience, focus, and true mental toughness.

I have found that when I keep my cell phone on silent, not vibrate, but silent, I am able to get more things done because my "flow" is not constantly interrupted.

I have found that when I consistently reach out and provide value to strangers on twitter that our influence grows, our business grows, and people are positively impacted (Except for the few that tell me to "F off and stop spamming them")

I have found that when I focus all my energy on the things inside my control I have more peace, confidence, and get better results.

I have found that as I intentionally focus on and developing true mental toughness that I attract more incredible people in my life.

I have found that as I am more consistent to talk to myself instead of listen to myself, I am more proud of my behavior.

I have found that as I fight to more consistently live by my principles instead of my feelings, I have burned fewer bridges, and have created more opportunities.

I have found as I am more consistent to say "No", I have more margin to say "Yes" to all the things that are most important in my life.

Consistency doesn't necessarily mean safe or boring. We can consistently choose to chase lions and choose the toughest challenges in life. Maybe consistency in your life looks like hustling on your dream and not watching your favorite TV show for a year. Maybe it looks like consistently showing up and being present for dinner with your family.

Sometimes it takes a long time before you see your consistency pay off. Maybe you are in a season of life where you took over a field that had almost no fruit and it looked a lot like a jungle. Maybe your heart is more like a jungle than a well-manicured garden.

All I know is that consistency creates fruit. The areas in your life where you see growth are the areas where you are consistent. We ask those we lead to be consistent, but the hard thing for us to do is to look in the mirror and figure out what we consistently are bringing to the table.

The storms in our life provide the greatest opportunity to develop consistency, and if we can be consistent in the midst of them, we are creating the foundation needed to sustain success.

Become consistent no matter if you have raging storms, or you are on the peaks of mountains. As Phil Jackson would always tell his team, "win or lose.....chop wood, carry water." In other words, become consistent and you will attract resources, opportunities, and people you never dreamed of.

CHAPTER 79

Stick To Your Principles

My initial reaction was to walk away.

My head was spinning.

"How could they do this?" I repeated to myself.

From the beginning of negotiations we agreed I would have ninety minutes to speak, and now with less than an hour before I was supposed to start, they told me I only had sixty.

The weather was beautiful, so maybe I would just go play golf instead of give the keynote.

I was seriously confounded about what to do.

Finally I typed up an email and told them I would be happy to only speak for sixty minutes but that I would be expecting my full rate instead of what I had agreed to contingent upon having ninety minutes to speak.

I hit send and walked to my car. As I drove to get breakfast my stomach was in knots.

Did I do the most beneficial thing?
Was I completely undercutting my message?
Was I a fraud?
Was I living out true mental toughness?

Then it hit me.

When a person in leadership calls me and tells me about a problem they are having I always tell them the same thing, "It's your problem. You have the power. Don't bitch, don't beg, enforce healthy boundaries with love and respect."

I took a deep breath and let it go. I had no clue what would happen, but I felt more confident in my choice to enforce the healthy boundary.

On my way back to the venue I checked my phone and sure enough, I had my thirty minutes back.

In his book *Procrastinate on Purpose,* my friend Rory Vaden discusses the idea of multiplying your time. He suggests we should spend our time on things today that will multiply our time in the future.

Enforcing healthy boundaries with love and respect is one of the ways you multiply your time in the future. Imagine how much more time and *energy* you would have if you started enforcing boundaries.

We spend so much energy battling people, begging, manipulating, and pushing to get them to do what we think is best instead of just enforcing healthy boundaries with love and respect right from the get-go.

Instead, most of us operate out of fear.

"I can't do that, this is my livelihood we are talking about!"

"I can't get her to follow the rules. She will quit, and she brings in more revenue than anyone on our team."

It can be terrifying to enforce healthy boundaries with love and respect, and we don't know what will happen. Most of the time I think the behaviors will change pretty quickly, but other times you will have to let someone go or they will quit.

The speaking engagement I referenced at the beginning of this chapter was one of my first in the corporate space, and when it was happening I couldn't believe it was starting off like that. Truthfully, I thought enforcing the healthy boundary could cause backlash and make it very challenging for me to get further opportunities in the corporate world.

Afterwards, I was so happy with the way I handled it. Not only did it make for a great story, but it reinforced my belief and experience with the benefits of enforcing healthy boundaries with love and respect.

When you start to hustle, you will have many opportunities to compromise your principles, and you might even get some short-term benefits from doing so. But long-term, you will erode your character and be much worse off practically-speaking as well.

My challenge to you is this:
Operate out of love.
Take back the power.
Relinquish the fear.
Create and enforce healthy boundaries with love and respect.
Live by your principles regardless of the cost.

"The reason we love and admire people like MLK, Ghandi, and Abraham Lincoln is not because they are extraordinary men with God-like qualities. We love them because they were ordinary people who were willing to die for living out extraordinary principles."

CHAPTER 80

The Illusion And Sexy Allure Of Partially Controllable Goals

This summer I traveled to Costa Rica with Steph. On our second to last night there, we came across a picture book with a stunning cascading waterfall. We woke up early the next morning, ate breakfast, checked out, and began a race against the clock to make it to experience the waterfall. The guy who sold us the book said it would take about five hours to get to it.

We pulled out of our hotel at 9:15 a.m. If it took us all five hours, we would arrive around 3 p.m. at the latest.

The fact that I was driving helped. The person at the rental car warned us not to drive like the "crazy Costa Rican drivers." However, he failed to realize that hard and aggressive driving is *my normal*. Our plan seemed simple enough: drive straight to our hotel, drop our bags, and then drive the last hour to the waterfall. Along the way we discussed whether we should see two waterfalls, and go back to the beach for sunset... *we thought we had time.*

Two hours into the trip, our GPS said we needed to go across a bridge for 24 km. We arrived at the "bridge" at 11:15 a.m. to our first sign of trouble. The "bridge" was a car ferry, and it didn't leave until 12:30 p.m. The thirty minutes of "crazy Costa Rican driving" I knocked off our trip was not only eaten, but on top of that we now had to wait an extra hour and fifteen minutes. We were now looking at an arrival closer to 4 p.m. We took some pictures by the beautiful ferry, and I tried to enjoy the view and the journey. Truthfully though, I wasn't enjoying the journey because my sole focus was achieving my goal (getting to the waterfall) and I wouldn't be satisfied until we (I) made it there.

I had a couple beers and took pictures to pass the time on the ferry. Determined to make it, we were the first people off the ferry, and we were once again racing to our destination. We hit a little bit of traffic and rain, which put us into our hotel at 3:30 p.m. Steph had guesstimated that it would take another hour max to get to the waterfall. We hadn't eaten anything since breakfast, but after the GPS said it would actually take closer to two hours to get to the waterfall, we grabbed a couple beers, skipped food, dropped our bags, and ran back to the car.

The GPS now said arrival at 5:25 p.m.
Sunset is at 5:40 p.m.
Every night we had paid attention to the sunset, and we knew we still had light until roughly 6:30 p.m.

As we drove, Steph asked me, "Do you want to go to the closer waterfall, or maybe even swing by the National Park, instead of the cascading waterfall?" I shrugged her off as if she'd just suggested we ride the mechanical horse outside a Wal-Mart instead of go on Pirates of the Caribbean at Disneyland.

We (I) were *going* to make it to the cascading waterfall.

Now Steph was driving, and I was once again trying to pass the time by taking pictures. I wish I could say I was enjoying the beautiful journey, but I wasn't. As I snapped photos, a notification popped up on my phone, "No more space for photos." I immediately went in and deleted an hour long video of a workshop. I then tried to snap another photo. Still, "No more space for photos."

"ARE YOU KIDDING ME?!" I yelled aloud.

Steph reminded me that iPhones sometimes need to be connected to wifi or a cell tower before the deleted video will register as cleared space. I immediately started frantically deleting text messages to see if that would free up space. It did. Determined, I began working my phone like it was a video game to clear as much space as possible for what were certain to be the most stunning photos of a cascading waterfall ever taken by a human being. Meanwhile I snapped at Steph every few minutes about her driving, or in response to anything she dared ask me while I was busy.

I picked my head up just as we made the turn for the waterfall. I knew I missed some stunning views on the ocean drive, but I knew it was all worth it because we were only 10km from the waterfall and I now had space for pictures and videos.

The GPS announced our arrival, but we saw nothing but a roadside stand.

It was 5:12 p.m.

I jumped out and ran to the stand, asking how to get to the waterfall. The young guy went to the back, and out came a woman I assumed was his mother.

Me: "How do I get to the waterfall?"
Her: "It's too late."
Me: "How do I get to the waterfall?!"
Her: "It's too late. Come back tomorrow."
Me: "We leave in the morning, and now is the only time! HOW DO I GET TO THE WATERFALL?!"
Her: "The waterfall is 6km away. It is about to downpour, and you can only drive 2km. The last 4km you must go by foot. It is a very bad idea. You can't make it there and back. There isn't enough light, it is very dangerous. You'll be in the middle of the rainforest with no one around to help you if you get in trouble."
Me: "I'm going, so how do I get there?!"
Her: "Turn right at the first road."

We jumped back in the car, and Steph was pleading both in words and

201

body language for me to listen to her, the tour guide, and the rapidly-diminishing sunlight, but it was a foregone conclusion. I traveled for over eight hours to experience *the* cascading waterfall, and it was too late now to turn back or admit defeat.

We passed the parking lot for the waterfall, and drove up all the way to the bridge where cars aren't supposed to go past for their own safety. I jumped out and put my backpack on, and asked Steph how her ankle was. She told me she wasn't going to let me go alone, so she tied her shoes and we started to run into the jungle.

I'm sure she asked if we could just stop and go somewhere else multiple times along the muddy last 2km road, but she might as well have been asking a statue, because I couldn't even hear her. As we crossed the first bridge, it started to rain. At least I stopped for ten seconds to get one photo of her running across the bridge.

Then I ran past her.

It was muddy and hard to get good footing after the bridge, but we pressed on. Occasionally, I looked back to see if I could still see her.

We passed one couple leaving.
We pressed on.
Another couple approached.

Me: "Is it worth it?"
Them: "Oh, it's amazing! But you'll never make it in time. And it's very dangerous."
Me: "Steph, walk back with them. I *have* to go!"

I took off running, harder now. It immediately started to rain buckets in the way only a rainforest can. I ran harder. I was now running through muddy trails made for horses. I came across a pond in the middle of the path, and I could barely get around it. I tried to make a mental note for my trip back in the dark. The light was getting worse. I kept running hard, though the hills in the rain and mud were making my legs burn. I got to the top of another hill and reality finally set in.

I could make it to the cascading waterfall, but then I would have no light for a difficult (even with sunlight) trek back.
I'm in the middle of a second-world country.
There are jaguars in this rainforest.
Steph is worried sick, on a partially sprained ankle, and I've abandoned her with a random Australian couple in the middle of the rainforest.
It is pouring rain.
It's almost 6 o'clock and my only sustenance for lunch was a liquid diet of beer.
The rainstorm is killing the last of the sunlight.

I am not going to reach my goal. I will not experience the cascading waterfall.

I screamed out a guttural animal sound at the top of my lungs. I cursed the rain and Costa Rica. *I sacrificed so much to achieve my goal, and I was less than 2km away, but I knew I needed to turn back.* I screamed and cursed it all again and… I finally turned around.

You'd think I would have learned the lesson by now. I literally wrote the book Burn Your Goals. Goals, even partially controllable ones like winning, rebounding, and sales, are so sexy and alluring, but even more dangerous. My focus was on the partially controllable goal, and I spoiled the journey, my character, my health, and my relationship in the process. I compromised the things that are not only important to me, but the things I spend my life trying to teach others to do well.

Cascading waterfalls in life are sexy and alluring, and I hope you get to experience some of them. But if we're focused on them instead of true mental toughness, we so often end up compromising all the things that truly matter. Sometimes we make it to the waterfalls, many times we don't. Regardless of whether we achieve our goal or not, there is always a path of destruction in our wake.

It is easier to justify the wake of destruction when you achieve the

goal, and even more of a reality check when you don't. I watch people do it every day in business and sports, and then I turned around and ran head first into the same illusion.

Maybe one day I'll learn.

"You can go chase a dream, but then sometimes you look back and there's a trail of tears behind you. And the tears are usually your wife and kids." — Mark Richt (Head Coach of Georgia Football).

CHAPTER 81

Someday

One of my friends growing up had a father who worked at an airplane factory. He didn't like his job, but it kept his family fed and housed while they went through school, and so he endured it. He punched in, did his work for eight hours a day five days a week, and then punched out. As a member of the factory workers' union, he quickly figured out the "system" designed to give its members a good life after retirement. He discovered that if he worked an extra day per week and took as few vacation days as possible, he could "bank" all that extra time toward pushing his retirement date earlier, all while saving the extra money for retirement itself.

And so, he began to work Saturdays as well. He missed his kids' soccer and football games, dates with his wife, family vacations, golf games with his friends, and even neglected the dream he once had for starting a small business of his own. He ended each week too tired to do much more than sit on the couch and watch TV. But he knew that it would all pay off someday, once he reached a certain age and cashed in all this time for his retirement. Once he did that, he'd have plenty of free time to spend with them, and plenty of money to afford to do the things he loved.

Days turned to weeks, turned to months, turned to years, and before he knew it, his career had passed in a blur. His kids were grown, several with children of their own now, and while he was one of the most well-loved employees at the factory, he still felt no more love for his work than he first did thirty years before.

But finally, he reached "someday." The big day arrived, and his family and friends all showed up for his retirement party. It was a wonderful evening. He couldn't be happier, and spent the night talking to everyone about how excited he was for his life to "really" start, now that he was retired and could do all the things he'd wanted to do for so many years.

He probably went to bed that night dreaming, for the first time in three decades, of waking up the next morning and starting a new week.

The problem is, he never did. He died in his sleep of a brain aneurysm instead.

This is one of the most terrible things I've ever experienced in my life, and not just because this man's death left my friend without a father, and his wife without a husband. It's terrible because he traded almost every single "today" for a "tomorrow" that he never got. He traded all of his dreams, and far too many of his memories with those he loved, for a future that he thought would be given to him.

But none of us are guaranteed "someday."

All we have is today.
All we have is our 1,440 minutes.
All we have is what we can do with the controllables in our life.

For a whole generation of American workers, retirement was the goal. And a whole generation made the same trade that my friend's dad did, giving away the best working years of their lives just to be able to play golf and cards with their friends one day.

But thank God, the rules have changed.

While there's nothing inherently wrong with golf, and certainly nothing wrong with using financial wisdom to save for the future, there is something truly evil about wasting your most precious resource each day at a job you hate, just to maybe "someday" waste even more time in retirement by doing nothing but playing around.

206

Don't be fooled: working at a job you hate is so much different from doing the hard, gritty, valuable work that is totally necessary to become great. Working at a job that doesn't require anything from you but button-pushing and boredom is *not* hustle: it's suicide.

Don't waste your life. None of us are guaranteed "someday."

All we have is today.

CHAPTER 82

The Man In The Mirror

The speech Al Pacino gives in the movie *Any Given Sunday* is one of my favorites, and my guess is that you have heard the "inches" speech at some point in your life.

In that speech he says, "It's the guy who is willing to die who is going to win that inch." You don't ever want to fight someone who is willing to die, because it's impossible to beat them. Same thing goes for fighting a crazy person. This is why any war in the Middle East is impossible to "win," because so many of the combatants are willing to die.

The person who is not willing to die in the fight ironically has a greater chance of dying. They are more likely to freeze up, not trust their training, react slower, and panic.

It's the person who is willing to die who has the greatest chance of survival. It's the person who is willing to fail who has the greatest chance of not failing. The person you want beside you in battle is the guy who has surrendered the outcome and is willing to die. The person you want on your team is the person who has surrendered the outcome.

You cannot control the outcome, and by trying to, you actually give yourself a greater chance of getting the outcome you do *not* want.

Think about relationships. If a person wants it too badly, they become needy and desperate, and they tend to push the other person away.

Success operates the same way. The more you focus on getting the outcome you want, the more you become your own greatest impediment to achieving it.

I believe the 5 keys to success are:

Operate with a perpetual heart posture of gratitude.
Commit to control the controllables.
Patiently and perpetually chop wood carry water.
Trust the process and God.
Surrender the outcome.

I think our biggest fear is often, "What if I absolutely exhaust myself and give my everything and it's not good enough?! What if *I'm* not good enough?!"

That is a possibility, and some people will never exhaust themselves beating on their craft to protect their fragile ego. My argument is that if you will surrender the outcome and focus on the fact that you are building your own house, you will eventually become the type of person who maximizes their potential. You will fail along the way, but failure is temporary, not permanent. *Failure is an experience, not an identity.*

Until you surrender the outcome, the person staring back at you in the mirror will always be your greatest enemy to your personal greatness.

CHAPTER 83

Born To Be Great

You were born to be great.
But you have been lied to.
The media wants you to believe that greatness is sexy, it's not.
It's dirty hard work.

You were born to be great, but some of you look in the mirror and all you can see are your flaws.

God made you perfectly. He doesn't make mistakes. *My brother can't walk talk or feed himself, but that isn't a mistake, or an accident.* He was created perfectly and meticulously for a purpose, and so were you and I.

You were born to be great, but some of you think all you have to do is just show up and bless the world with your presence.

You matter. Your value comes from who you are, *not* from what you do.

But most of you will never become everything you were created to be because you either can't believe you truly have greatness inside of you, or you think it's just supposed to fall on top of you!

When I was living in that gym closet, I had to look at myself in the grungy mirror every morning and genuinely believe that I was becoming the leader of a world-changing organization. If I had never changed how I saw myself and what I spoke over myself, then I never would have be come the person of influence and opportunity that I am today.

If I was just a dude living in the closet of a gym, that impacts what time I get up, how I treat people, what I read, how I work, and what I do.

You are where you are because of what you *believe*, how you *think*, and what you habitually *do*.

Opportunities exist all around us, and will continue to do so. But most people either can't even see them, or simply repel them based off of their character.

How would you hustle today if you knew you were going to get the opportunities of your dreams in 6 months, 2 years, or 4 years?

Once the opportunity comes, it is too late.

A few months ago the biggest sports training academy in the world contacted me and asked me to head up their mental conditioning and leadership department.

I told them no.

Three months went by and they reached out and asked again, because they looked all over the country and said they couldn't find anyone better than me.

I told them no again.

I don't say that to brag. Five years ago, I got turned down for entry-level jobs at Target, Starbucks, and Enterprise Rent-a-Car.

But for the last five years, I've been beating on my craft and hustling my face off. I wasn't interested in getting a sport psychology degree. I don't have one. This is bigger than a degree. I'm becoming the leader of a world-changing organization.

The guy interviewing Jamie at the sports academy said, "People have spent decades studying, working, and training, and you guys have more influence and opportunities than they do. How does this happen?!"

You know how this happens? *We weren't trying to get a job.*

And guess what? *We still aren't trying to get a job.*

We are focused on becoming the best in the world at inspiring, equipping, and training people. Our mission has been and continues to be to love people, serve people, and provide value.

Too many people are worried about getting a starting spot on the team, or getting that job, getting an A in a class, or completing that project for their boss, but they're completely missing the bigger picture.

It's not about the job, it's about you!
It's not about your team, it's about you!

It's not about your employees, it's about who you become!
It's not about your customers, it's about who you become!
It's not about your dream, it's about who you become!

If you started to understand that it's not about today, then you would care so much more about what you do today.

If you truly understood the greatness inside of you, if you truly saw in yourself what God sees in you, you would stop messing around with parties, drugs, TV, mindless activities, video games, foolishness, and anyone in your life who is intent on keeping you from becoming everything you were created to be.

If you actually took yourself seriously, you would do radically different things with your time.

If you really wanted it as bad as you say you do, then you would do radically different things with your time.

No one gets more than 86,400 seconds in a day, so how you use your most precious resource greatly impacts who you become.

It's not your boss' responsibility.
It's not your coach's responsibility.
It's not your parents' responsibility.
It's your responsibility.

It's not about today!
So stop getting caught up in today's drama.

"My boss doesn't like me."
"Another VC group said no."
"My teacher doesn't like me."
"My team sucks."
"It's not fair."

So. What.

It's not about today!

Why not? *Because the only thing that matters about what you are doing today is who you become in the process.*

The only thing that matters about what you are doing today is the impact you have on other people.

Stop being average!
Stop just getting by on "good enough"!
Stop blaming other people!
You were born to be great!
Start acting like it!

The obstacles in front of you are there to build you into the person you are destined to become, but you keep running from all the obstacles!

When are you going to realize they aren't obstacles, they are a training ground for greatness?!

Stop running from your problems, and start embracing them!

Do me a favor. The next time you get cheated on, say to yourself, "<u>Yes</u>! Thank you for the opportunity to become greater!"

The next time your computer freezes and you lose all your work, say to yourself, "<u>Yes</u>! Thank you for the opportunity to become greater!" The next time your boss gives you a seemingly impossible assignment, say to yourself, "<u>Yes</u>! Thank you for the opportunity to become greater!"

The next time you get benched, say to yourself, "<u>Yes</u>! Thank you for the opportunity to become greater!"

Strength is only built through resistance.
Greatness is only built through trials.
Diamonds are only formed under pressure.
Gold is only refined through fire.

Do me a favor, and get excited about everything life throws at you! Start saying "yes" to everything most people say "no" to, and start saying "no" to everything most people say "yes" to!

There's a scene I love in *The Dark Knight Rises* where Bane says to Batman, "Victory has defeated you." Some of you think that you are just going to show up and say, "I'm Joshua Medcalf," and we think life is just going to lay down and give us what we want because of our degrees, or our grades, or our family, or our talent, but it won't!

Batman cuts off the lights because he thinks he has an advantage in the dark, and Bane says, "The dark? You trained in the dark, you adopted the dark. I was born in the dark, molded in the dark, shaped in the dark."

The temptation is to let victory defeat you. I had my degree from Vanderbilt. I basically had my master's from Duke. My family had money at that point. I could have lived in my family's home in Tulsa. I could have lived in one of our two condos in Playa del Carmen, but I knew that I had massive dreams, and in order to give myself a chance, not a guarantee, but a chance to become the type of person who could achieve those massive dreams, then I couldn't let victory defeat me.

Stop letting victory defeat you!
I know that for most of you, you were born in the dark. You went through hard stuff to become who you are today, and in order to become who you want to become you are going to have to go back and embrace the dark for a little while longer.

Most people are seeking out the bright lights, and they think that all they need are the bright lights to show the world their greatness. But be careful you don't get exposed by the light.

Are you willing to hustle, train, and sacrifice in the dark for five to ten long years?! Most people are seeking out the safe, comfortable, and cool job, but rarely is that going to be the place that molds you and shapes you into an unstoppable force!

The greatest predictor of future success is the ability to delay gratification. But I promise you, a lot of people were laughing when I didn't write my master's thesis. A lot of people were scoffing when I moved into a homeless shelter. A lot of people were snickering when I moved into the closet of a gym. A lot of people were talking behind my back when I was reading for twelve hours a day and hustling on Twitter.

But they aren't laughing anymore.

The path to greatness isn't through the land of ease and comfort. *The Navy SEALs* intentionally seek out the toughest training environments in the world, because they know that on the other side of that training is greatness!

So stop running from the tough stuff! Instead, start seeking out and embracing the toughest challenges and you will be shocked at who you become.

215

If you will consistently and deliberately seek out and embrace the toughest challenges in life, if you will hustle in the dark for five or ten solid years, if you will beat on your craft, I promise that you will wake up one day in the distant or not-so-distant future, and realize you have become the person of your dreams.

"It is from numberless diverse acts of courage and belief that human history is shaped. Each time a man stands up for an ideal, or acts to improve the lot of others, or strikes out against injustice, he sends forth a tiny ripple of hope, and crossing each other from a million different centers of energy and daring, those ripples build a current that can sweep down the mightiest walls of oppression and resistance." — Bobby Kennedy

CHAPTER 84

"They" Will Try And Kill You In The Process

We pretty much come out of the womb creating and exploring. Ever notice how young kids often get more enjoyment out of the boxes than the toys?

But then we start school and we are told to sit down, shut up, and get in line. And then we wonder why obesity is an epidemic. We wonder why we lack initiative and creativity.

If you don't do what "they" say, they call you disobedient, unassimilated, disturbed, or worse, they diagnose you with ADHD. Then they drug you, all to get you to fit in their nice little box. We were created to explore, create, love and learn.

If you put one crab in a bucket, it will crawl out. If you put multiple crabs in a bucket, they will pull each other down every time one starts to crawl out. *If a crab continues to try and crawl out of the bucket, the other crabs will break its leg.*

We live in a society of crabs.

They called John Wooden crazy when he tried to run a press for the entire game. They also thought it was crazy that he didn't scout opponents; rather, he chose to focus on letting the other team worry about stopping his team.

The board at Apple ran Steve Jobs out of the company calling him crazy and reckless. Twelve years later, just months away from bankruptcy, they came crawling back begging him to come back and save them. He took Apple from the fringes of bankruptcy to one of the most successful and innovative companies of all time.

A massive oak tree comes from a single persistent nut. You have to be crazy to change the status quo. It's not supposed to be easy. But you weren't created to sit still. You were created to be unique, not to fit into a box. **Be careful who you get advice from. Many people have a vested interest in seeing you fail. If you succeed and show that it's possible, then they no longer can say it's "impossible."**

"They" wanted to have the person committed who came up with the idea of television. "They" thought the idea of a 24-hour sports network was stupid and could never work. "They" called Nelson Mandela a terrorist. "They" called Jackie Robinson unthinkable names. Rest assured, "They" will call you all sorts of names, they will throw down the gauntlet in front of you, they will do everything they can to keep you inside their "safe" container.

Be courageous. Once you break out they will call you a genius, and tell everyone how talented you are. They will try and neatly sweep all your years of sweat, turmoil, and uncommon persistence under the rug. It's so much more comfortable to believe talent is reserved for the chosen few, than it is to work your ever-loving ass off and hustle to become the best you are capable of being.

CHAPTER 85

Don't Die With It Trapped Inside!

Most people die with their greatness inside of them, because they were more worried about failing and being embarrassed than they were about being courageous enough to keep hustling.

Most people die with their potential trapped inside of them.

Most people die with their dreams trapped inside a garage or a computer because they believed the lie that it wasn't good enough, a lie which eventually strangled the dream.

I want you to be different.

I want you to die knowing that you exhausted yourself and you gave it everything you had.

Someone is depending on you.

Maybe you will change the world.

Maybe you won't, but I guarantee that you will change someone's world, and that *that* someone might change the whole world.

If you don't dig deep and find the courage to live your dream, then you are setting everyone in the world back. It may not be perfect, and it may not even be great yet, but don't let that stop you from getting it out there and into the hands of those who need it most. Don't let that stop you from consistently hustling in the dark.

You can continually make it better, but *don't let the enemy trick you into believing it isn't good enough and no one needs it.*

We need it.
The world needs you.
We need you to create it, ship it, and ultimately become who you are destined to become.

Please don't die with your potential trapped inside of you because you believed the lies.

Hustle.
Exhaust yourself.
Hustle.
Beat on your craft.
Chop wood. Carry water.
Fall in love with the process of becoming great.
Become so great they can't ignore you.

Ready To Start Applying Everything You Learned?

Go to **t2bc.com/hustlebook**
to download your **free** action plan today!

Additional T2BC Resources

Keynote Speaking- Email Joshua@traintobeclutch.com

Mentorship Program- Our mentorship program isn't a good fit for everyone, but we are always willing to see if it is a good fit for you. It is a serious investment of time and resources. Email Joshua@traintobeclutch.com for more information.

T2BC Reading Challenge- t2bc.com/challenge to sign up for free today

The Experience- *Transformational Leadership Retreats*. We bring together people from all over the country to engage in a day of interactive learning. We also create space for fun activities like golf, surfing, or snowboarding with Joshua and Jamie. Visit **t2bc.com/experience** for more information and to see when the next retreat will be.

T2BC 101 Online Video Course- With over 20 short video sessions, you can use this course individually or to teach your team the T2BC curriculum. It is a great next step tool. Available at **t2bc.com/training**

Join the T2BC community- This is the best way for us to provide consistent value to your life and for us to develop a long term relationship.

You will get articles, mp3's, videos, and other tools as they come out. It's also free. ☺ Join **at t2bc.com**

Books- You can always order signed copies of any of our books by emailing us, and they are also available on iBooks, Kindle, Amazon, and through our publisher at **Blurb.com**

The first book we wrote is ***Burn Your Goals.***
The second book we wrote is ***An Impractical Guide to Becoming a Transformational Leader.***
The third book I wrote in conjunction with this book is, ***Chop Wood Carry Water***, which is a fable that brings the T2BC curriculum to life in a memorable narrative. Originally it was all one book, but eventually I decided it would be better to have two separate books.

YouTube- Our channel is train2bclutch

Twitter- @joshuamedcalf

Instagram- @realjoshuamedcalf

Website- t2bc.com

Thank You's From Joshua

I'm incredibly grateful to my mother, who has supported me and been one of my best friends my whole life. Thank you for never giving up on me when no one would have blamed you if you had.

Thank you to my father, who did the best he could with what he had.

Thank you Judah Smith for being the most amazing pastor a person could ask for. You have taught me so much about Jesus, how He really feels about me, and how I can live like Him. I don't think anyone has ever had such a profound impact on my life in such a short period of time as you have.

I'm so grateful to Jamie and Amy, you both have been such an amazing support system in my life, and I'm so grateful I get to spend so much time with you. Thank you for creating a safe space for me to be me devoid of judgment.

Thank you Amber for always listening to my stories. It's pretty amazing to hear about how you have grown so much in the last couple of years.

Thank you to Austin, TJ, Kyle, Joe, Pooter, Krause, Brady and my many other friends who have been there for me during the many low points in my life.

Thank you to Tim & Laura for being a living representation of the love and grace of Jesus!

Thank you Anson for all your words of encouragement, and for allowing me to work with your program.

Thank you Steph for being an amazing woman full of love, empathy, and creativity. Your childlike spirit encourages and inspires me every day. Your sunshine lights up the world.

Thank you Lisa for always being there to hear my articles, or just to listen to another one of my crazy stories, and for being an incredible best friend!

Thank you Russ and Skip for all the mentorship over the years. Thank you Skip for being one of the first people outside of my family to financially invest in me and my dreams.

Thank you Andy and Terry for teaching me so much as a teenager. I wouldn't be here today without your love and wisdom.

Thank you Jacob Roman for clearing your schedule to transform my horrific grammar and at times incoherent thoughts into something people will love and treasure!

Thank you Thom for editing the first very rough draft!

Thank you to all the people who have given me the great privilege and responsibility of mentoring you and speaking into the lives of those you lead. I have learned so much, and I am truly grateful for the opportunity to work with you.

Thank you to Tim McClements for never giving up on me at Vanderbilt, and helping me get a scholarship at Duke. I was a royal pain in your ass, and I'm forever grateful you stuck by my side.

Thank you Adri for all your prayers and friendship.

Thank you Jesus for your extravagant, reckless, relentless, and undeserved love.

CPSIA information can be obtained
at www.ICGtesting.com
Printed in the USA
BVOW09s2059120517
484026BV00002B/98/P